Copyright for Library and Information Service Professionals

Second edition

INFORMATION MANAGEMENT

Published by Aslib, The Association for Information Management and Information Management International
Staple Hall
Stone House Court
London EC3A 7PB
Tel: +44 20 7903 0000
Fax: +44 20 7903 0011
Email: *aslib@aslib.co.uk*
WWW: *http://www.aslib.co.uk/*

ISBN 0 85142 432 5

Copyright for Library and Information Service Professionals

Second edition

Paul Pedley

INFORMATION MANAGEMENT

Is your organisation a corporate member of Aslib?

Aslib, The Association for Information Management, is a world class corporate membership organisation with over 2000 members in some 70 countries. Aslib actively promotes best practice in the management of information resources. It lobbies on all aspects of the management of, and legislation concerning, information at local, national and international levels.

Aslib provides consultancy and information services, professional development training, conferences, specialist recruitment, Internet products, and publishes primary and secondary journals, conference proceedings, directories and monographs.

Further information is available from:

Aslib, The Association for Information Management
Staple Hall
Stone House Court
London EC3A 7PB
Tel: +44 20 7903 0000
Fax: +44 20 7903 0011
Email: *aslib@aslib.com*
WWW: *http://www.aslib.com/*

Series Editor

Sylvia Webb is a well-known consultant, author and lecturer in the information management field. Her first book, *Creating an Information Service*, now in its third edition, was published by Aslib and has sold in over forty countries. She has experience of working in both the public and private sectors, ranging from public libraries to national and international organisations. She has also been a lecturer at Ashridge Management College, specialising in management and interpersonal skills, which led to her second book, *Personal Development in Information Work*, also published by Aslib. She has served on a number of government advisory bodies and is past Chair of the Information and Library Services Lead Body which develops National Vocational Qualifications (NVQs) for the LIS profession. She is actively involved in professional education with Aslib and the Library Association and is also a former Vice-President of the Institute of Information Scientists. As well as being editor of this series, Sylvia Webb has written three of the Know How Guides: *Making a charge for library and information services*, *Preparing a guide to your library and information service* and *Knowledge management: linchpin of change*.

A complete listing of all titles in the series can be found at the back of this volume.

About the author

Paul Pedley is Head of Research at the Economist Intelligence Unit. Previously Paul was Library & Information Services Manager at city law firm Theodore Goddard, where he worked for 6 ½ years. He has also worked in property libraries (for Olympia & York Canary Wharf Limited, the developers of Canary Wharf in London's docklands) and in government libraries (for the Department of Trade and Industry, OFTEL, and the Property Services Agency).

Paul is a Fellow of the Library Association, an active member of a number of professional groups including the Library Association's Industrial & Commercial Libraries Group, and a past chair of both the Property Information Group and the City Law Librarians' Group. He is currently a special libraries representative on the Library Association Copyright Alliance.

In addition to writing *Copyright for library and information service professionals*, Paul has written *Intranets and push technology: creating an information sharing environment*, which is also published as an Aslib Know How Guide. He has written a number of articles for journals such as the *Library Association Record*, *Business Information Review*, *Internet Newsletter for Lawyers*, and *Information World Review*; and speaks at professional meetings on topics ranging from copyright, competencies of special librarians or networking to whether the internet could and should be regulated.

Contents

Abbreviations

AAHSL – Association of Academic Health Services Libraries

AALL – American Association of Law Libraries

ALA – American Library Association

ALCS – Authors' Licensing and Collecting Society

ARL – Association of Research Libraries

BCC – British Copyright Council

BLDSC – British Library Document Supply Centre

CBI – Confederation of British Industry

CDPA – Copyright, Designs and Patents Act

CLA – Copyright Licensing Agency

CLARCS – Copyright Licensing Agency Clearance Service

DOI – Digital Object Identifier

DTI – Department of Trade & Industry

EBLIDA – European Bureau of Library, Information and Documentation Associations

EC – European Commission

ECMS – Electronic Copyright Management Systems

ECUP – European Copyright User Platform

EFPICC – European Fair Practices in Copyright Campaign

elib – Electronic Libraries Programme

ERA – Electronic Redistribution and Archiving

EU – European Union

GATT – General Agreement on Tariffs and Trade

HERON – Higher Education Resources ON-demand

HMSO – Her Majesty's Stationery Office

IARs – Information Asset Registers

ICOLC – International Coalition of Library Consortia

JISC – Joint Information Systems Committee

LA – Library Association

LISLEX – Legal issues of concern to the library and information sector (in *Journal of Information Science*)

MLA – Medical Library Association

NESLI – National Electronic Site Licence Initiative

NLA – Newspaper Licensing Agency

PA – Publishers Association

PDF – Portable Document Format

PLS – Publishers Licensing Society

SLA – Special Libraries Association

TRIPS – Trade-Related Aspects of Intellectual Property Rights

UCC – Universal Copyright Convention

WIPO – World Intellectual Property Organisation

Introduction

Only one thing is impossible for God: to find any sense in any copyright law on the planet. Mark Twain, Notebook, 23 May 1903.

Copyright is a property right which arises automatically on the creation of various categories of work, and protects the rights and interests of the creators of literary, dramatic, musical, and artistic works, sound recordings, films, broadcasts, and cable programmes and the typographical arrangements of published editions.

Copyright is a complex field. The legislation is changing rapidly in order to take account of technological change. As each of the new technologies has made multiple copying easier and faster, rights holders have successfully lobbied for copyright protection to be strengthened. To operate effectively, the information society requires balanced copyright laws. Governments need to ensure that the economic rights of information providers are balanced with the needs of users to gain access to information. This has been achieved by providing for exceptions, such as fair dealing and library privilege. Article 9.2 of the Berne Convention[1] says that

'It shall be a matter for legislation in the countries of the Union to permit the reproduction of such works *in certain special cases, provided that such reproduction does not conflict with a normal exploitation of the work* and *does not unreasonably prejudice the legitimate interests of the author.'*

1

In other words, there are three steps involved:

- step 1: for special cases only
- step 2: should not conflict with a normal exploitation of the work
- step 3: does not unreasonably prejudice the legitimate interests of the author.

Under the Berne convention, the WIPO Copyright Treaty, the TRIPS agreement and the draft EU copyright directive, all exceptions to copyright must pass the three-step test as outlined in the Berne Convention Art. 9.2.

In the UK, the use of exceptions to balance the rights of copyright holders against the rights of users of copyright material has been put under considerable strain. Exceptions such as fair dealing and library privilege do not apply equally to information stored in both paper and electronic formats. For example, the concept of fair dealing has been watered down, so that the copying of databases for commercial purposes cannot be considered to be fair dealing.

Library and information service professionals are often called upon to administer copyright compliance within their organisations. They may be seen as the expert on what is and is not allowed, or be the administrator of copyright licences with organisations such as the Copyright Licensing Agency or the Newspaper Licensing Agency. Very few library & information service professionals are qualified as lawyers, and yet we are the ones who are called upon to navigate the increasingly complex copyright maze. I do not claim to be an expert on copyright law, but I am a librarian who has to deal with copyright issues on a day to day basis; having to apply the legislation on copyright in live situations. This means that in my work I am consulted on whether certain copying is permissible, dealing with questions such as:

- Is it alright for me to make 10 copies of this article?

- Do we have a licence for copying newspapers?

- Can I photocopy the article which you printed out for me from database X, and send it out to the client?

- Am I allowed to make a complete copy of this consultation document?

Copyright infringement is actionable by the owner of the copyright, who may seek damages and / or injunction, and is also a criminal offence under the Copyright Designs and Patents Act 1988 (CDPA) which carries on conviction a fine and/or imprisonment for up to two years. To date the Copyright Licensing Agency (CLA) has not had a criminal prosecution, but organisations which undertake infringing behaviour are therefore running the risk of becoming the subject of a test case.

The Copyright, Designs and Patents Act 1988 is the main statute on copyright. It radically overhauled legislation in the area of intellectual property, and took account of developments since the previous Copyright Act of 1956. However, there have been a number of significant technological developments since the publication of the CDPA

1988, and as a result some of these have been taken account of through subsidiary legislation.

Anthony Trollope said 'take away from English authors their copyrights, and you would very soon take away from England her authors'[2.]

Economic Rights

Copyright in a work entitles the copyright owner to five main economic rights. These are:

- copying the work
- issuing copies of it to the public
- performing it or playing it in public
- broadcasting it or including it in a cable programme
- adapting it.

Moral rights

People tend to concentrate on econmic rights, but authors also have a number of moral rights. Sections 77-89 of the CDPA 1988 deal with moral rights. These are:

- the right of paternity
- the right of integrity
- the right of false attribution
- the right of disclosure.

The right of paternity (ss77-79) is the right of the author to be identified as such. According to section 78 infringement of the right of paternity does not occur unless the right of paternity has been asserted. That is why many publications contain statements such as:

'The right of Paul Pedley to be identified as the author of this work has been asserted by him in accordance with the Copyright, Designs and Patents Act 1988'

or 'Paul Pedley has asserted his right under the Copyright, Designs and Patents Act, 1988, to be identified as the author of this work'.

The right of integrity (ss80-81) – the right of the author to prevent or object to derogatory treatment of his/her work.

The right of false attribution (s84) – the right of persons not to have a literary, dramatic, musical or artistic work falsely attributed to them.

The right of disclosure (s85) – the right of the author to withhold certain photographs or films from publication.

Duration of copyright

The duration of copyright was changed as a result of SI 1995/3297: *The Duration of Copyright and Rights in Performances Regulations 1995* which came into force on 1 January 1996.

Literary, dramatic, musical or artistic works

If the author is a European Economic Area (EEA) national, then copyright expires 70 years after the end of the year of an author's death. Copyright always expires on 31st December, i.e. the end of the calendar year.

Crown copyright

Items are protected for a maximum of 125 years. However, if the work is published commercially during the first 75 years of that time, then the protection is for 50 years. (Crown copyright covers works made by Her Majesty or an officer or servant of the Crown in the course of his/her duties such as a civil servant or an employee of a government agency.)

Parliamentary copyright

50 years from the year in which the work was created. (Parliamentary copyright exists in work commissioned by either House of Parliament.)

Databases

When a database attracts copyright protection the usual rules of duration of copyright for literary works apply. For those databases which do not qualify for full copyright protection as compilations but do qualify for database right, protection is given against unfair extraction and reutilization for 15 years.

I think that all library & information service professionals would recognise the intellectual property rights of authors and publishers, and that they would want to do everything they could to respect those rights. Indeed, a number of librarians are authors of books and articles in their own right. I also think, though, that copyright legislation must be workable. There has to be a balance between respecting the property rights of authors & publishers on the one hand, and on the other hand the practical needs of employees in business, local and national government, and other institutions to copy material in order to get on with their day to day work. In practice library and information professionals have to walk along a delicate tightrope between rights holders and information users. We have to comply with an ever more prescriptive regulatory regime, whilst attempting to satisfy the information needs of library users. It is not a case of information professionals trying to avoid paying royalties to authors and publishers. Rather, it is a case of wanting a practical framework within which to operate, where bureaucratic procedures are kept to a minimum. We need to lobby for a regulatory framework which respects the interests of both rights owners and information users, and achieves this in a way which avoids creating an unworkable bureaucratic nightmare.

The British or common law tradition considers copyright to be a piece of property, which can be traded as a marketable commodity. In essence, copyright is about making sure that authors and publishers get fairly paid for their work. Authors and publishers are therefore not in the business of reducing or restricting access to the product of their labours, unless that proves to be a necessary measure in order for them to protect their livelihoods. There is a very clear connection between the value and the cost of information. As more information is made available through electronic means, the true costs of organising, storing and retrieving information are becoming higher and higher; and the costs are also becoming highly visible. People are starting to realise that information is a commodity, and that nothing is ever really 'free'.

Whilst the author has taken care in verifying the information contained in this guide, no liability can be accepted for errors or omissions.

1. Copyright and libraries

Librarians have a pivotal role to play in the implementation of copyright legislation. By the very nature of their work they are placed between on the one hand the authors, publishers and other copyright owners who quite rightly are keen to obtain a fair economic return on their intellectual property whilst on the other hand they deal directly with the readers of copyright works. Library and information professionals therefore have a key role in both controlling and facilitating access to information, and as such they also have to be able to explain to their users what levels of copying are permissible under copyright legislation.

This unique role which library & information professionals have is recognised to a limited degree in the copyright legislation. Sections 37-43 of the CDPA 1988 give certain librarians explicit permission to make copies for their users. The Act gives them protection against copyright infringement, provided they comply with a number of bureaucratic procedures to earn that indemnity. This is known as 'library privilege'. However, there are a number of major drawbacks of which library and information professionals should be aware.

Library privilege applies only to not-for-profit libraries[3], so industrial and commercial libraries are not covered. In practice the privileges only seem workable for paper-to-paper copying. Whilst there is no reason in theory why library privilege should be limited to paper-based copying, the problem is that librarians are required to see that the requestor signs a copyright declaration form and the question of getting digital signatures has never been satisfactorily resolved in this regard.

Governments need properly to acknowledge the pivotal role which librarians have as intermediaries in the information chain by providing exceptions to copyright which would allow library and information professionals to make a limited amount of copying of data in *all* formats on behalf of their users, by clearly and explicitly extending the scope of exceptions such as those on fair dealing and library privilege.

The author understands that some librarians have been put under pressure by their employers to make infringing copies, with the threat of disciplinary proceedings if they refuse to comply. Members of the Library Association who are put in this situation should remember that the LA has a code of professional conduct which says:

'Members must fulfil to the best of their ability the contractual obligations owed to their employer. However circumstances may arise when the public interest or the reputation of the profession itself may be at variance with the narrower interests of an employer. If it is found to be impossible to reconcile such differences then the public interest and the maintenance of professional standards must be the primary considerations.'[4]

My advice to any library & information professionals who are put into this sort of dilemma, would be to approach their professional body to talk through the situation in confidence. Employers who do put pressure on librarians to break copyright law should recognise that they may well be storing up trouble for themselves which will surface at a later date. A legal action brought by the Copyright Licensing Agency was made possible because a disaffected librarian rang a whistleblowers' line operated by the CLA to alert them to copyright infringement which was occurring at their former place of employment.

Librarians may not be popular in pointing out which copying is and is not allowed within the regulatory framework, but in practice they are the people who have to administer copyright at the sharp end. How often have you been asked whether or not a particular course of action is acceptable, and have had to make a decision based upon your interpretation of copyright law?

Rights holders are defending their intellectual property rights more vigorously than ever before. For example, the Copyright Licensing Agency, which is responsible for looking after the interests of rights owners in copying from books, journals and periodicals refers to its Copywatch campaign as the 'CLA's "get tough" approach' on copyright infringement[5], and elsewhere speaks of Copywatch as 'the [CLA's] aggressive anti-copyright theft campaign'.[6]

Some people believe that copyright clearance of in-house copying is a tiresome and, in some cases, impracticable operation. They argue for a one-stop shop which would license organisations for all their in-house copying, regardless of format. It is highly unlikely that such a body would ever be set up in practice, although librarians and information professionals would obviously welcome the blanket licence approach, as it would make things so much simpler. To save the need for individual permissions, rights owners have formed a number of collective licensing schemes. However, they are not comprehensive and in order to comply with their licences, users have to check that the journals, newspapers, books and so on are covered by their licences. The problem is particularly acute in the area of electronic information. The CLA, for example, has only recently introduced a digitisation licensing programme, and the licences which are currently available cover only a few sectors – the higher education and the pharmaceutical sectors; and are limited to the production of an exact electronic facsimile of an existing printed page. They do not cover digital publishing, such as CD-ROMs or online publishing. Many library and information professionals must therefore rely on the subscription contracts or conditions of purchase that they have with each provider of electronic information. When they wish to undertake copying where permission is required, they have to seek out the rights owners who may well not be interested in making the effort to deal with individual requests for permission to copy particular items, and may not even respond to requests from information professionals who are doing their best to comply with the law; or else the rights owners may allow the copying to be under-taken, so long as a prohibitively high fee is paid.

Librarians will wish to demonstrate that they are taking reasonable steps to comply with copyright legislation. So, what actions can they take to achieve this?

Staff handbook

Some firms have a written policy on copyright, drafted in accordance with the CDPA 1988. In a number of organisations, this written policy state-ment forms part of the terms and conditions of employment.

Posters

Libraries with photocopiers for use by readers need to take particular care to ensure that they have not unwittingly authorised the making of infringing copies. Posters reminding staff of the permitted lim-its for the photocopying of documents restricted by copyright can be displayed next to all photo-copiers within a firm. For example, both the Library Association and Aslib produce posters intended for display beside photocopying machines; whilst the Copyright Licensing Agency provides licence hold-ers with photocopier warning notices as well as copies of their Excluded Works and Categories List to display prominently next to photocopiers.

Clear labelling on items not covered by the licences

Where an organisation has taken out licences under the various collective licensing schemes, library staff might wish to put some sort of notice onto books and journals which are not covered by the licence and/or onto pamphlet boxes containing magazines which are not covered by the licence.

Notes on the library catalogue records of items not covered by the licences

Another step which librarians may wish to consider is to put a general note onto the catalogue records of publications which are not covered by the copyright licences which the organisation has taken out. When a library user searches for material on their chosen topic, they would then be prompted if any of the items fell outside the scope of the firm's copyright licences.

I am sure that some people will consider this to be impractical. But how do you ensure that an organisation is complying with the copyright regime when the licences available are not blanket licences? Indeed the licences certainly do not cover all publishers, all publications, or material from all countries of the world.

Appointing a key contact for copyright queries

A number of organisations direct queries about copyright matters to a named individual. This person acts as a central point of reference for all members of staff within the company who have any questions about making copies of material which is protected by copyright. The CLA licence requires there to be a licensing administrator who is responsible for the day-to-day operation of the licence.

2. User permissions

The two main exceptions to copyright as set out in the Copyright, Designs and Patents Act 1988 are *fair dealing* and *library privilege*. These exceptions permit some copying for the purposes of research or private study.

Fair Dealing

Section 29(1) of the CDPA 1988 deals with fair dealing for the purposes of research or private study. It says: 'Fair dealing with a literary work, other than a database, or a dramatic, musical or artistic work for the purposes of research or private study does not infringe any copyright in the work or, in the case of a published edition, in the typographical arrangement.'

Regulation 8 of the Copyright and Rights in Databases Regulations 1997 (SI 1997/3032) inserted subsection 1(A) 'Fair dealing with a database for the purpose of research or private study does not infringe any copyright in the database provided that the source is indicated'.

The problem is that the Act does not define what is meant by the phrase 'fair dealing'. It is therefore left for the courts to decide whether or not a particular instance of copying is fair, based upon the individual merits of the case. This point is made in an important case which pre-dates the current Act, where Lord Denning emphasised that what is fair will depend on the particular circumstances of the case.[7]

Whilst the CDPA 1988 does not spell out what is meant by fair dealing, it does give some guidance as to what fair dealing is not.

Section 29(3) says 'Copying by a person other than the researcher or student himself is not fair dealing if .... (b) .... the person doing the copying knows or has reason to believe that it will result in copies of substantially the same material being provided to more than one person at substantially the same time and for substantially the same purpose.'

In other words, multiple copying undertaken on another person's behalf for the purposes of research or private study cannot be considered to be fair dealing.

The phrase 'fair dealing' is commonly thought to mean that the copying would not unfairly deprive the copyright owner of income for their intellectual property. The Copyright Licensing Agency explain very clearly what they understand the phrase 'fair dealing' to mean:

'Fair dealing means dealing fairly. It cannot, therefore, from the common meaning of the words, be fair dealing to steal someone else's work, or to deprive them of their just income. Copyright owners - the authors and publishers of copyright material, earn income not just from sales of the original, but also from copying permission fees and photocopy licensing schemes such as that operated by CLA in the UK. This income is a just return for the creative work of the author and the financial investment made by the publisher. If the copying deprives the copyright holder of money, however small the amount may be, it is stealing: and stealing is not fair. *If it is not fair, it is not fair dealing'*[8].

Section 29(5)[9] says 'The doing of anything in relation to a database for the purposes of research for a commercial purpose is not fair dealing with the database".

Fair dealing is effectively a 'defence" against accusations of infringement rather than a licence to copy. Fair dealing only applies to three specific purposes:

(i)   research or private study s29(1)

(ii)   criticism or review s30(1), provided that it is accompanied by a sufficient acknowledgement

(iii)   reporting current events s30(2), provided that it is accompanied by a sufficient acknowledgement. In the case of reporting current events, the fair dealing defence does not cover photographs.

The British Copyright Council[10], which represents the UK's authors and publishers, has agreed that in the case of books, a 'reasonable proportion" means the greater part of one chapter or five percent of the book. The BCC's advice on this point only applies to books. It does not apply to the making of a single copy of a whole journal article, and many publishers consider that the copying of a complete journal article is not fair dealing. The BCC has also said that whilst poems and short stories are themselves complete literary works, that authors and publishers would regard as fair a single copy of a whole poem or short story, not more than ten pages long, published in a book.

Library Privilege

Library and information professionals working in 'prescribed libraries' should familiarise themselves with The Copyright (Librarians and Archivists) (Copying of Copyright Material) Regulations 1989 (SI 1989/1212). These regulations were made under the CDPA 1988 ss37-43, and came into force on 1 August 1989. The regulations give special privileges to certain libraries and archives under copyright law; and they apply to library staff who carry out photocopying on behalf of their users and for other libraries. In contrast to the vagueness of the fair dealing provisions, the CDPA 1988 outlines 'library privileges' very precisely which gives certain librarians protection against copyright infringement, provided that the procedures have been followed correctly. Librarians are therefore in a unique position under the Act, having complete indemnity - but they have to comply with various bureaucratic procedures in order to earn that indemnity.

Libraries are permitted to make single copies of individual articles in a journal to their patrons; the law states that they may never supply more than one copy to the same patron, or copies of more than one article from the same issue of a journal to the same patron, but in real terms this is impossible to police. CDPA 1988 s37(2)(a) says that the librarian can rely on a signed declaration form, unless he is aware that it is false. The law defines an 'article' as 'any item', so you should regard an Editorial, an individual article, a letter to the Editor all as articles. Thus, if you have supplied one article to an individual you cannot then supply him or her with a copy of another article from the same issue. Strictly speaking the contents page of a journal counts as an article, which would clearly have implications for current awareness services. The Library Association's guidelines for industrial and commercial libraries[11] states that 'it is the view of the LA that circulating journal contents pages is a way of advertising the journals and does not necessarily damage the economic rights of rights holders. There are some publishers who agree with our view and do not see this practice as encouraging copyright infringement, but other publishers disagree'.

Libraries can only be 'prescribed libraries' provided that they are not for profit. A full list of the libraries covered is given in Schedule 1 of the 1989 regulations. These libraries are 'prescribed' for the purposes of supplying a copying service to the public under ss38, 39 and 43 and for copying for archival or preservation purposes covered by ss41-42 whether within their own stock, made for another non-profit based service, or received from any other library.

Figure 1. Library Privilege

CDPA 1988 s38 allows a librarian of a prescribed library to make and supply a copy of an article in a periodical for a person; and

CDPA 1988 s39 permits a reasonable proportion of a literary, dramatic or musical work other than an article in a periodical to be copied [library privilege does not cover artistic works]

so long as the following prescribed conditions are complied with:

(a) that the requester signs a form (of the type set out in the Schedule to the Library Regulations SI 1989/1212 – see figure 2) declaring that:

- a copy of the same material has not previously been supplied by any librarian;
- the material is for the purposes of research or private study only
- the requester is not aware that any other person has requested or is about to request a copy of substantially the same material for substantially the same purpose

(b) that the librarian does not fulfil requests for substantially the same material at substantially the same time

(c) that no more than one copy of an article per periodical issue or no more than a reasonable porportion from a published work is requested; (reasonable proportion is undefined)

(d) that the librarian makes a charge for the copy to recover the costs of production, including a contribution towards the general expenses of the library

The librarian or archivist of a prescribed library or archive is permitted to make a copy from an item in the permanent collection of the library or archive

(i)   in order to preserve or replace that item by placing the copy in a permanent collection in addition to or in place of it, or

(ii)   in order to replace in the permanent collection of another prescribed library or archive an item which has been lost, destroyed or damaged when it is not reasonably practicable to purchase a new copy.

A 'prescribed library' is a not-for-profit library, meaning one that is neither established for profit itself, nor part of an organisation established for profit. This includes public libraries; national libraries; libraries in educational establishments; parliamentary and government libraries; local government libraries; other libraries [any library which encourages the study of bibliography, education, fine arts, history, languages, law, literature, medicine, music , philosophy, religion, science (including natural and social science) or technology; and any library outside the UK which encourages the study of the above subjects].

The Declaration form must be substantially in accordance with Form A in Schedule 2 to the Library Regulations SI 1989/1212

Figure 2. Declaration: Copy of article part of published work

To:

The Librarian of ....Library
[Address of Library]

Please supply me with a copy of:

* the article in the periodical, the particulars of which are
[   ]

* the part of the published work, the particulars of which
are [   ]

required by me for the purposes of research or private study.

2. I declare that –

(a)   I have not previously been supplied with a copy of
        the same material by you or any other librarian;

(b)   I will not use the copy except for research or private
        study and will not supply a copy of it to any other
        person; and

(c)   to the best of my knowledge no other person with
        whom I work or study has made or intends to make,
        at or about the same time as this request, a request
        for substantially the same material for substantially
        the same purpose.

3. I understand that if the declaration is false in a material
particular to the copy supplied to me by you will be an
infringing copy and that I shall be liable for infringement
of copyright as if I had made the copy myself.

† Signature..

Date ....

Name ....

Address..

....

* Delete whichever is inappropriate

†This must be the personal signature of the person making the request. A stamped or typewritten signature, or the signature of an agent, is NOT acceptable.

3. Licensing schemes

Normally if someone wishes to exploit copyright material beyond the limitations of statute law, they need to get permission by approaching the copyright owner directly. For librarians and information professionals who are regularly making use of a wide range of copyright materials from literally hundreds of different publishers it would be totally impractical for them to have constantly to make contact with the rights owners. What we really need is a truly 'one-stop shop'. Until such time as a body is set up to license companies and organisations for *all* their copying, the clearance of in-house photocopying remains a tiresome and, in some cases, impracticable operation. To save the need for individual permissions, rights owners have formed a number of collective licensing schemes. These organisations act collectively for groups of copyright owners in respect of particular rights, and they may offer 'blanket' licences to users, although the term 'blanket' is somewhat misleading, as the terms of the licence would be very strictly defined.

In the past few years, many commercial organisations have entered into licences with collective licensing bodies representing the publishers of newspapers and periodicals to permit the taking of multiple copies of press cuttings and articles for distribution within the organisation or even to its clients.

The problem is that these licensing schemes certainly do not represent a truly 'one-stop' shop, and it is doubtful whether such an organisation could ever be set up in practice. The licences do not cover every publication within their chosen category of material. The Copyright Licensing Agency, for example, maintains a regularly updated list of works which are excluded from their licence. This means that there is an onus on the librarian to check if the magazine or journal article or the section of a book to be copied is excluded from the licence. The schemes could only cover all publications if the rights holders were forced to participate by statute, and in the UK this is considered to be an unreasonable extension of government power over rightsholders.

The 1988 Copyright, Designs and Patents Act encourages the use of the law of contract for collective licensing. Contract law can override copyright law, and in the case of any dispute in licensing schemes the Copyright Tribunal, set up by the 1988 Act, can arbitrate on the terms and conditions of the licensing schemes.

Copyright Licensing Agency

The Copyright Licensing Agency is the UK reproduction rights organisation. It was founded in 1982 by publishers and authors to license education, government and business in order to allow them to photocopy copyright books, journals and magazines. The CLA is a not-for-profit company which is owned by the Publishers' Licensing Society and the Authors' Licensing & Collecting Society. The licence fee is then used to compensate owners of intellectual copyright for the use of their work. Payment of the licence fee also protects businesses from prosecution under the Copyright, Designs and Patents Act (1988) provided that the licence is complied with.

'The typical CLA [business] licence permits the making of an agreed number of copies (the number can vary according to the fee paid) of up to one article from a periodical and journal or one chapter of a book (or 5 per cent of the publication whichever is the larger) for an annual fee based on the number of students or professional employees in the organisation concerned. If required, further copying can be carried out of either more material from one publication or copies in excess of the number permitted by the licence, for an additional fee, as long as the rightsholder has mandated the CLA to give this additional permission. This service is called CLARCS'[12] (see page 28).

The key elements of a CLA licence are outlined in figure 3. The licence covers a basic limit of 9 copies of an item. But it is possible for an additional fee to choose a higher limit of 19 or 29 copies.

The CLA operates Copywatch, an aggressive anti-copyright theft campaign to crackdown on unlicensed copying, and has a hotline for those who have confidential information about illegal copying. It vigorously defends the rights of authors and publishers, and is prepared, where necessary, to instigate legal action against copyright infringers, which can result in substantial fines for the perpetrators (see chapter 9 - case law).

Speaking before the launch of Copywatch, the CLA's then Chief Executive, Colin Hadley said: 'Illegal copying is the most common crime in the UK today. 8 out of 10 people admit to copying illegally in the workplace. As a consequence authors and publishers are being deprived of millions of pounds in royalties and lost sales. This cannot be tolerated. Our new Copywatch campaign will use all the latest investigative techniques to expose copyright theft in local and national government, schools and colleges, as well as business'[13].

The CLA licence provides licence holders with an indemnity, provided that the terms of the licence have been complied with. This would mean no excluded works copying, no excessive copying, and no illustrations copying. Collective licensing schemes are required under the CDPA 1988 to provide such indemnity: s136 of the Act is headed 'Implied indemnity in schemes or licences for reprographic copying'.

The Copyright Licensing Agency provides a central copyright clearance service to licence holders. This facility is known as CLARCS, the CLA's Rapid Clearance Service. This service is only available to organisations in possession of a current CLA licence. Under the standard CLA licence, organisations are normally licensed to make up to 9 photocopies of extracts from books, journals and periodicals. If they need to make 10 or more photocopies of any extract, copies of more than one article from an issue of a periodical or more than one chapter of a book, then the CLARCS service exists to provide a quick method of gaining copyright clearance. Some copyright holders may not permit any copying above the 9 copies permitted within the normal CLA licence.

Table 1: key features of CLARCS

Clears additional copying for
- course packs
- internal copying
- document supply

Clearance can be obtained over the telephone or by fax.

Publishers may set own fees for different types or exclude some or all works

The CLA received £1,026,094 income from CLARCS in 1998/9 of which £484,057 came from the business sector[14]

Table 2: Default CLARCS rates

	(internal)	(document delivery)
Books per page	£0.13	£0.25
Journals per article	£2.50	£4.98
Magazines per page	£0.10	£0.18

These are the rates the CLA suggests but publishers can set their own. There is also a higher education flat rate for course packs of 5p, irrespective of book, journal or magazine.

The CLA's whole purpose is to collect fees for copying, and in doing so they aim to avoid spending pounds in order to collect pennies. In other words they try to collect and distribute fees in an efficient way, keeping administrative costs in check. It is also of vital importance that the fees collected are then distributed in a fair way. To do this, licence holders are required to undertake an information audit as part of their annual licence agreement. It is quite likely that the library or information manager will be nominated as the 'Information Auditor'. The information which the CLA needs to know as part of the audit includes:

- what journals your organisation subscribes to
- how many copies of each are normally received
- how many issues there are per year
- which ones are free
- what controlled circulation / individual subscription journals are received
- what new books have been purchased in the past 12 months.

Library and information professionals should be aware that in taking out a licence with the CLA, that they will have to allocate a certain amount of time in order to fulfil the requirements of the licence, especially the need to complete a regular information audit. It is perfectly understandable that such information is required in order to ensure that the copyright fees which the CLA has collected are distributed fairly, but librarians should not underestimate the work involved in administering a CLA licence.

'The fees which the CLA collects are passed over, after deduction of a 10 per cent subvention to cover the CLA's running costs, to the Publishers' Licensing Society and the Authors' Licensing and Collecting Society, for onward distribution to their members. Distributions are based on the results of CLA surveys of what copyright material is being copied in licensed institutions and businesses. Accumulating and processing such survey data is a significant part of the CLA's activities but it is essential to achieve a fair and statistically valid basis for the distribution'[15]. In 1997-98 gross revenue was £19.2 million, and distribution of copying fees to rightsholders was £16.1 million.

Table 3: CLA Copyright Fee Distribution

Books = 50% to ALCS, 50% to PLS

Serials = 100% to PLS

EXCEPT in future for

- serials in course packs, where publisher has not claimed to own 90% or more of rights in literary content (ALCS 25% / PLS 75%)

- out of print books (ALCS 85% / PLS 15%).

Figure 3. The standard CLA business licence

Currently costs £7.50, £15, or £22.50 per professional employee per annum, depending on which business sector you are in

Permitted

Copying from certain magazines, journals and books only

Paper-to-paper copying only is permitted (ie. No electronic copying of any sort)[16]

Permits you to take up to nine copies of up to one article from an issue of a periodical whenever you want during the licence year

The CLA's Rapid Clearance Service is available to business licensees wishing to make more than nine copies

Copying from publishers originals only (not photocopies or faxes)

Not permitted

Copying more than one article or one chapter or one law report or 5%

Copying magazines or books which are on the CLA list of excluded works

Maps, charts, books of tables, music, newspapers, bibles etc.

Separate photographs, illustrations, or diagrams

Electronic capture, storage, or re-use or faxing

Commercial use or re-publication

Works published in certain territories are excluded

Public examination papers, privately prepared teaching materials

Industrial house journals

Newspaper Licensing Agency

The Newspaper Licensing Agency Limited (NLA) was established in January 1996 by the national newspaper publishers so that any company, firm, or other organisation wishing to copy from newspapers for internal management purposes could easily obtain the permission it needs to do so lawfully. The Agency distributed copies of its booklet entitled *Photocopying newspapers: your guide to the new rules*[17] which is now in its seventh edition and known as *Copying newspaper cuttings – a general guide to the rules*. This outlines the types of licence available from the NLA, to bring companies, firms and other bodies within the law.

According to the NLA, permission is needed to make multiple copies or send faxes of articles from newspapers. However, I think that in certain circumstances the sending of a newspaper article by fax could be said to be permitted without a special licence. So long as the article was sent for a legitimate purpose, and that neither the sender nor the recipient had kept a copy in electronic format for permanent storage, then I believe that the retention of a single paper-based copy does not infringe copyright.

The NLA provides a choice of two main forms of direct licence, known as Form A and Form B.

Form A ('Application for and grant of indemnity and licence for photocopying and faxing of cuttings from newspapers')

'So that licensees may avoid having to count every single copy made and keep accurate records of this, Form A allows unmonitored ad hoc and systematic copying in return for a fee based on the size of the licensee and an estimate of the volume of systematic copying likely to be carried out over a year'.[18]

Form B

Form B requires the licensee to count carefully and declare to the NLA quarter by quarter the actual number of copies made, so that the quarterly fee can be calculated. The licensee may also be required to demonstrate to the NLA that it has adequate internal systems to ensure that all copying is properly recorded.

Fee structure

The Newspaper Licensing Agency has a leaflet entitled *Simple guide to applying for an NLA licence* July 1999 which outlines the fee structure for their licences. Basically, for licence Form A, PA or HEA the fee is made up of four components:

1.Basic charge for copying

This is based either on the number of staff or the turnover of the organisation as well as the number of newspapers in the supplemental UK and foreign repertoires to be covered by its licence (see figure 5).

2. Systematic copying

This is the number of copies made systematically during the tally period (usually a fortnight) annualised and charged at the prevailing tariff [currently 2.066p per copy for UK newspapers or 5p per foreign newspaper].

3. Indemnity fee

The NLA was set up in January 1996. Anyone applying for a licence is required to pay an indemnity fee for past copying to cover the period from January 1996 to when the licence is taken out.

4. VAT

VAT is added to all fees.

With Form B, the charge is 2.066p per copy made of each cutting copied for UK newspapers or 5p per copy made from foreign newspapers, subject to a minimum quarterly fee of £31.

For library and information professionals wishing to take out an NLA licence, I would strongly recommend Form A rather than Form B. The requirement of Form B that a daily log is kept of all photocopies made from newspapers is an administrative headache. If you work in a firm which has, say, 30 photocopiers or which has 3 UK offices, it would be extremely difficult to ensure that all copying was being recorded onto a tally sheet, showing newspaper by newspaper the number of photocopies which had been made each day.

No licence is required by the client of a press cuttings agency if the agency itself has an NLA licence and if the agency makes all the copies of cuttings that its client requires. But if the client makes *ad hoc* copies, or runs an internal clippings service or makes further copies of clippings supplied by its agency, the client does require a licence.

The NLA licence would normally only cover the use of copies for internal management purposes. But there is a special form of licence, Form PA, which permits professional practices to occasionally provide their clients with copies of cuttings.

In addition to having the basic licence, the Newspaper Licensing Agency also has special licences for professional practices (form PA), public relations consultancies, schools, and other educational establishments (form HEA) and charities.

Figure 4. The Newspaper Licensing Agency licence

Copying from certain newspapers only.

Paper-to-paper copying only is permitted (ie no electronic copying of any sort unless the NLA has granted an electronic extension to the licence).

No copying of photographs and advertisements.

Copying permitted for management information purposes only, ie no copying for:

– distribution internally to a sales force for use as a sales aid

– inclusion in an in-house publication

– inclusion in the company's annual report and accounts

– marketing or promotional purposes

– inclusion in a book

– inclusion in any other publication, such as a newspaper or a magazine.

A maximum of 250 copies of any one article.

With Form PA for professional practices copies can be distributed to clients and other business contacts, so long as they are under cover of a letter signed by the fee earner for no more than 10 addressees.

Figure 5. Publications covered by the NLA licence

The Newspaper Licensing Agency has three lists of newspapers covered by their licence. The publications lists or repertoires are divided into national UK papers, regional UK papers (the supplemental UK repertoire), and US newspapers. When people apply for a licence, they will automatically be covered for the UK national papers on the NLA's list; but if they want their licence to cover items listed on the other repertoires, they must complete *Form SLIST – the Newspaper Licensing Agency Limited supplemental UK repertoire and foreign repertoires* identifying which titles the licence should cover.

Publications covered by the NLA licence

National repertoire

Daily Mail

Daily Star

The Daily Telegraph

Evening Standard

The Express

Financial Times

The Guardian

Independent

Independent on Sunday

The Mail on Sunday

The Mirror

News of the World

The Observer

The Sun

Sunday Express

Sunday Mirror

Sunday People

The Sunday Telegraph

The Sunday Times

The Times

Supplemental UK repertoire

The Bath Chronicle

Birmingham Evening Mail

The Birmingham Post

The Coventry Evening Telegraph

Daily Record

Derby Evening Telegraph

Edinburgh Evening News

The European

Evening Express (Aberdeen)

Evening Post (Bristol)

Evening Times

Grimsby Evening Telegraph

The Herald

Hull Daily Mail

International Herald Tribune

Lancashire Evening Post

Leicester Mercury

Manchester Evening News

Nottingham Evening Post

Press & Journal (Aberdeen)

Scotland on Sunday

The Scotsman

Scunthorpe Evening Telegraph

The Sentinel (Stoke-on-Trent)

South Wales Evening Post

The Star (Barnsley edition)

The Star (Doncaster edition)

The Star (Rotherham edition)

The Star (Sheffield edition)

Sunday Business

Sunday Herald

Sunday Mail

The Sunday Mercury (Birmingham)

Western Daily Press

Western Gazette

Western Morning News

Yorkshire Evening Post

Yorkshire Post

United States repertoire

Asbury Park Press (NJ)

Asian Wall Street Journal

Atlanta Journal and Constitution

Baltimore Sun

Christian Science Monitor

Columbian (Vancouver, WA)

Dallas Morning News

Evening Sun (Baltimore, MD)

Federal Times

Grand Prairie News (TX)

Hartford Courant

Irving News

Los Angeles Times

Miami Herald

New York Newsday

New York Times

News Tribune (Asbury Park, NJ)

Orange County Register

Philadelphia Daily News

Philadelphia Inquirer

Richardson News (TX)

San Francisco Chronicle

Star-Ledger (Newark, NJ)

Wall Street Journal (all US editions)

Wall Street Journal Europe

Washington Post

NB. This list was correct at the time of writing. For an up-to-date list, please check directly with the Newspaper Licensing Agency.

Copyright Tribunal

The Copyright Tribunal is an independent body established in 1989 under the Copyright, Designs and Patents Act 1988 (sections 145-152) to settle various types of copyright disputes, mainly in the field of collective licensing. 'It has the statutory task of conclusively establishing the facts of a case and of coming to a decision which is reasonable in the light of those facts. Its decisions are appealable to the High Court only on points of law. (Appeals on a point of law against decisions of the Tribunal in Scotland are to the Court of Session')[19]. The Patent Office website maintains details of cases currently before the Tribunal and details of decisions issued.

HMSO

The trading businesses of the former HMSO were sold to the National Publishing Group on 30 September 1996, trading as The Stationery Office Limited. Whilst the whole of HMSO was privatised, the Controller of HMSO undertook certain functions on behalf of the Crown which were not undertaken by Parliament or any nominated government department. Consequently, a small residuary body, known as Her Majesty's Stationery Office, remains within government and operates as a Division within the Machinery of Government and Standards Group of the Cabinet Office. The division continues to be headed by a Controller. Her Majesty's Stationery Office is responsible for the administration of Crown and Parliamentary copyright and for overseeing certain Queen's Printer functions.

The Copyright Unit of Her Majesty's Stationery Office produces a number of advice notes on the photocopying of Crown and Parliamentary copyright material. There are advice notes for publishers, librarians and civil servants. These notes can be found on the Internet at http://www.hmso.gov.uk/copy.htm (accessed 13.3.2000). Her Majesty's Stationery Office does not operate a licensing scheme in the way that organisations such as the CLA and NLA do. In fact, the HMSO Copyright Unit says that 'users registered with the Copyright Licensing Agency (CLA) need not apply for permission to HMSO's Copyright Unit to photocopy Crown or Parliamentary material which falls within the terms of their CLA licence'[20]. Through the publication of a 'Dear Librarian' letter, the Copyright Unit of Her Majesty's Stationery Office provides guidance for library and information professionals wishing to photocopy, for local or personal convenience, modest amounts of Crown or Parliamentary material, and to clarify the range of photocopying which can be done without charge and without the need to seek formal permission. The latest version of the Dear Librarian letter is the 4th edition, dated 23 September 1996. The key points of the letter are summarised in figure 6.

A green paper[21] was published in January 1998 setting out a number of options for the future management of crown copyright. The green paper does not, however, deal with parliamentary copyright. This was the subject of a House of Lords written question[22] on whether Her Majesty's government would support a review of the management of parliamentary copyright in the light of their review of the management of crown copyright. The reply given by Lord McIntosh of Haringey was that 'the responsibility for the management of parliamentary copyright rests with parliament. A review of parliamentary copyright is, therefore, entirely a matter for senior parliamentary officials'.

A white paper[23] was issued in March 1999. This outlines the government's plans to improve access to official documents and make the licensing of material produced within government more streamlined and coherent.

Following the publication of the white paper, there has been a roll-out of guidance to place policy on access and re-use of crown copyright protected material in its full practical context. So far the following guidance notes[24] have been issued:

No. 1 *Copyright in typographical arrangement*

No. 2 *Reproduction of crown copyright scientific, technical and medical articles*

No. 3 *Copyright in public records*

No. 4 *Reproduction of court forms*

No. 5 *Copyright in works commissioned by the crown*

No. 6 *Reproduction of United Kingdom, England and Wales secondary legislation*

No. 7 *Guidance on copying birth, death and marriage certificates*

No. 8 *Reproductiion of national curriculum material and literacy and numeracy strategy documents for England*

No. 9 *Reproduction of government press notices for England, Northern Ireland and Wales.*

At the time of the publication of the white paper on crown copyright, the government launched *inforoute*[25]. This is a UK government web site which provides a gateway and central information point to guide and direct a route through the maze of official government information and materials. The responses to the green paper revealed a sense of frustration at the difficulty of locating government information. *Inforoute* is also intended to provide direct access to the government information asset registers (IARs) which list unpublished information such as datasets/databases and other significant information resources.

Other licensing schemes

For library and information professionals, the most important collective licensing schemes are those operated by the Copyright Licensing Agency and the Newspaper Licensing Agency. There are other licensing schemes in operation such as the one available from Ordnance Survey. If anyone wants to know more about the other licensing schemes available, these are mentioned in the Library Association copyright guidelines[26] and Graham Cornish's[27] book.

Figure 6. Her Majesty's Stationery Office 'Dear Librarian' Letter – Key Points

Permitted

Material which may be photocopied without prior permission or charge:

Hansard, Bills, Journals of both Houses, Lords minutes, Vote Bundles, Commons Order-Books, Public Bill and SI lists, Weekly Information Bulletins and Sessional Information Digests, Command Papers, Reports of Select Committees, Acts, Statutory Instruments, Statutory Rules and Orders, Press Releases.

For publications listed above, users are permitted to copy the text from any single title or document in their entirety provided that:

– no more than one photocopy is made for any one individual

– copies are not distributed to other individuals or organisations.

An exception is made for schools and places of higher education who are allowed to provide a single copy to each student.

Users are also permitted to make unlimited multiple copies of extracts from any single title or document provided that the extracts from any single

---

work do not exceed 30% or one complete chapter or equivalent, whichever is the greater.

For other Crown and Parliamentary copyright material, apart from those specified above, the user is permitted to make one copy of a single chapter or of 5% of an entire work, whichever is the greater.

Not permitted

Volume of copying beyond that listed above.

Making photocopies for advertising or endorsement purposes.

Reproduction which is made for the purpose of personal gain or commercial profit.

Reproduction in any circumstances which, in the view of the Copyright Unit, are potentially libellous or slanderous of individuals, companies or organisations.

Other points

If in doubt, ask.

4. Digital use of copyright material

We need to work together as a profession towards defining a model whereby electronic information delivery and storage can be exploited fully by libraries and end-users of information to improve access whilst protecting the rights of copyright holders from infringement. The overriding aim would be to permit use of information whilst monitoring this and ensuring that copyright owners are properly compensated for it.

Copyright protects the legitimate rights of the rights owners, but this should not frustrate technical developments or access to information. Anthony Julius says 'the history of copyright is the history of a struggle. Authors complain that their interests are inadequately protected; audiences complain that their access to author's work is unduly fettered. Authors both need, and are mistrustful of, their audiences. The relationship between authors and audiences is thus one of unhappy mutual dependence'[28]. Implementing copyright is a matter of balance, but commercial interests should not be allowed to prevail at the expense of access to information.

In an ideal world there should be a one stop shop or central agency to act on behalf of publishers in granting digital rights. But that is a utopian ideal. In the real world, the commercial interests of individual publishers make it extremely unlikely that we would ever get to the point where there was a collective licensing agency covering electronic databases such as CD-ROMs, online and Internet services. Others take a more optimistic view stating that the collective licensing schemes will evolve to meet subsidiary demands which cannot be met by primary rightsholder-licensee licensing; but that they cannot evolve until the primary market has itself become more established.

The Copyright and Rights in Databases Regulations 1997 SI 1997/3032 certainly open up the way for a collective licensing scheme covering electronic information, as they provide for licensing of database right and extension of the jurisdiction of the Copyright Tribunal to hear and determine proceedings relating to the licensing of database right.

What we need is straightforward and unambiguous licences. A way forward would be the development of a model contract between publishers and user groups. Here, there are grounds for optimism. Chapter 6 deals with the licensing of electronic resources.

Definition

Copying a literary work is defined as reproducing it in material form, including storing it by electronic means (see CDPA s17(2)).

CDPA s17(6) says 'copying in relation to any description of work includes the making of copies which are transient or are incidental to some other use of the work'.

The Copyright Rights in Databases Regulations 1997 SI 1997/3032 inserts into the CDPA 1988 section 3A which says

'...'database' means a collection of independent works, data or other materials which -

(a) are arranged in a systematic or methodical way, and

(b) are individually accessible by electronic or other means

... a literary work consisting of a database is original if, and only if, by reason of the selection or arrangement of the contents of the database the database constitutes the author's own intellectual creation'

Under these regulations, a database is only protected by copyright if there is creativity in its selection or arrangement. Otherwise it is protected by database right.

Fair dealing

Fair dealing is not clearly defined in law. It is generally thought to refer to restricting the amount of material which can be copied or used fairly so as not to damage the economic interests of rights owners.

Although rights such as fair dealing do apply to electronic works as well as to paper ones, in practice all accesses to online services need to be paid for.

The Copyright and Rights in Databases Regulations 1997 [SI 1997/3032], which came into force on 1 January 1998, insert into s29 of the CDPA the following words:

s29(1A) Fair dealing with a database for the purposes of research or private study does not infringe any copyright in the database provided that the source is indicated.

s29(5) The doing of anything in relation to a database for the purpose of research for a commercial purpose is not fair dealing with the database.

Any research using databases which is for a commercial purpose cannot therefore be considered to be fair dealing. This is the first time that UK legislation has distinguished between academic, scientific or commercial research. I am told that the commercial/non-commercial distinction was included in the Bill which became the CDPA 1988, but that it was excluded by the then government following strong representations from the CBI.

Library Privilege

Library privilege under sections 38 and 39 of the Copyright, Designs and Patents Act is limited to the making of *single* copies for the purposes of research or private study. In the past, a number of copyright experts argued that this effectively restricted library privilege to photocopying since electronic copying necessarily requires firstly, at least one copy for electronic storage and then at least one copy in the act of downloading.

However, regulation 9 of SI 1997/3032 introduces new section 50D containing specific exceptions to the exclusive rights of the copyright owner which permit any person having a right to use a database to do any acts that are necessary for access to and use of the contents of the database without infringing copyright.

In fact, regulation 9 inserts section 50D(2) which says: 'Where an act which would otherwise infringe copyright in a database is permitted under this section, it is irrelevant whether or not there exists any term or condition in any agreement which purports to prohibit or restrict the act (such terms being, by virtue of section 296B, void).'

There is nothing which says that library privilege only covers paper-to-paper copying. So, there is an implicit permission to copy electronic information under library privilege. However, the CDPA 1988 lays down very clear procedures which must be followed if the copying is done using the library privilege exception. These procedures include the completion of a copyright declaration form by the library user, and the whole question of digital signatures has never been satisfactorily resolved to the point where librarians can feel that they are fully indemnified.

Online and CD-ROM databases

The downloading of information from online databases is governed by the terms of the licence from the information provider under a subscription or service contract. These differ from database to database. Some providers, such as Dialog have a system of higher fees for copyright clearance, which would allow the user to import database records into an internal system for permanent storage in return for an agreed fee.

When signing up for access to an online database, or when purchasing a CD-ROM, end-users will normally sign a contract which will explicitly describe in the small print precisely what is allowed in terms of reproducing information retrieved. The printing out, copying, downloading or networking of CD-ROMs is therefore governed by the specific conditions of the licence agreements. It will normally exclude the selling-on of information to third parties and be explicit about the permitted uses of information retrieved by the subscribing organisation.

If licensing agreements between online hosts and database providers are satisfactory, the originator of the information will receive a fee each time that their data is accessed, covering the copy being made. This can of course be easily monitored through the same system as provides the billing information to the customer. The case of CDs is less simple and a one-off licence fee is usually built in to the subscription price, though some services have a device attached such as a dongle which limits the amount of information which can be downloaded or printed off from each issue of the disc.

The Internet

The information superhighway has made it possible for searchers to surf through millions of pages of material in a matter of seconds in order to obtain photographs, journal articles, reports, conference proceedings, overhead projector slides, annual reports and so on. Technological advances have made access to information far quicker and simpler than ever before. But, information which is accessed on the Internet is subject to copyright law just as printed sources are.

If you wish to copy information from a web site, you should first look at the page's own copyright notice. The page may have a notice which states clearly whether you can cut and paste, download, or print out material and, if so, how extensively. If there is no copyright notice, or if the copying you wish to undertake is not covered by the notice, you should obtain specific permission. This can probably best be achieved by emailing the webmaster for that particular web site.

Some web sites have used the technology in order to control what can be done. For example, a number of web sites do allow pages to be printed out, but they have disabled the 'cut and paste' or 'save as' functions; so that if anyone attempts to use those commands, they find that the buttons have been greyed out.

The Copyright Licensing Agency says that 'The World Wide Web is subject to copyright, and Web pages are themselves literary works. The textual articles contained on Web pages are also separate literary works, the graphics are artistic works, and any sound files are sound recordings containing separate musical works. In a single World Wide Web page there can be dozens of different copyrights. The consent of the copyright holder is required for each act of copying'[29].

There have been a number of legal actions concerning the practice of hyperlinking to other web sites. In the UK, for example, the Shetland Times case (see chapter 9 - case law) was all about the question of whether it was possible to include hyperlinks from your own site which link to another person's site. Since the case was settled out of court, no legal precedent was set.

The ability to hyperlink is the fundamental concept upon which the World Wide Web operates. However, as a matter of courtesy I would advise anyone who wishes to set up hyperlinks to other sites to get the permission of the copyright holders of those sites. Hyperlinking without that permission has caused people to get upset for a number of reasons:

- linking to a page other than the 'home' page may mean that people using the hyperlink do not see advertisements on the home page which actually fund the development and maintenance of the site

- the use of frame technology may allow you to create a link to another person's site, but because of the use of inline images (ie frame technology) it looks to the casual observer as though the information is part of your page and they may not be aware that they have now jumped to a totally different site.

Material from books, journals or periodicals should not be posted on the Internet or to newsgroups or bulletin boards without the written consent of the copyright holder.

With the swift advances in technology that we have witnessed in recent years, one wonders whether the law can effectively keep up with those technological developments. Is it possible to have a workable intellectual property law when on the one hand the Internet is global and on the other hand intellectual property is territorial?

Email

Technology makes it possible to send an email which can reach potentially hundreds of recipients across the world at the press of a button, and the recipients may themselves forward or copy the email to yet more people. Care must be taken when sending published information in digital format as an attachment, because unless you have a licence agreement which specifically covers the sending of such material to particular individuals outside your own organisation, you are in danger of infringing copyright.

The Norwich Union 'cyberlibel' case highlighted some of the legal pitfalls which organisations need to be aware of if their employees have access to the Internet or to an in-house email system. Western Provident took legal action when it was discovered that Norwich Union was circulating damaging and untrue rumours on its internal email system to the effect that its competitor was in financial difficulties and was being investigated by the DTI. The case was settled when Norwich Union publicly apologised in the High Court to Western Provident Association and agreed to pay them £450,000 in damages and costs.

Electronic Copyright Management Systems

As well as making and storing electronic copies, computers can be programmed to monitor and to ensure proper payment for the use of copies. These monitoring systems are called Electronic Copyright Management Systems (ECMS). Various ECMS are currently being developed.

Digital Object Identifier (DOI) System

International book and journal publishers have sponsored the development of an identification system for digital media. The International DOI Foundation held its first DOI Technology Forum on 10 December, 1997 at which Carol Risher said that

- copying could be prevented using restrictive file formats and limiting opportunities for download
- files can be encrypted and access sold based on either CD-ROM or network technologies

- encrypted files can be shared with a clearinghouse to collect usage data and fees[30]

DOIs can be attached to books, articles, abstracts, charts and so on. Clicking on a DOI takes searchers straight to the owner of the intellectual property concerned. They are used to authenticate content, and to reassure the creator of the information that the copyright in the content is protected. There are plans to use the DOI as the basis for electronic copyright management systems. The DOI will be the foundation of a number of rights management and rights trading systems

Scanners

The scanning of copyright works is illegal unless permission has been obtained from the copyright owner. Copying should be restricted to the following types of material:

- works for which your organisation holds the copyright, such as correspondence
- works which are in the public domain
- works for which the copyright has lapsed

Content access management

The key to devising a fair system of managing electronic copyright is technology. To avoid the copyright infringement of electronic information, publishers are looking to content access management or to put it bluntly 'put it where they can't copy'. There are a number of technological devices for ensuring copyright compliance. They include:

- watermarking
- dongles
- machine specific software
- passwords
- offline metering
- online metering.

The Copyright and Rights in Databases Regulations SI 1997/ 3032

The regulations came into force on 1 January 1998. The key points are:

- the regulations implement EC Directive 96/ 9/EC on the legal protection of databases which harmonises the copyright protection of databases in the EU

- databases which, by reason of the selection or arrangement of their contents, constitute the author's 'own intellectual creation' are specifically protected by copyright

- a free-standing *'database right'* was created for databases which do not satisfy this creative test. This right is a property right. It is an investor's rather than a creator's right: the first owner is the person who has taken the initiative and made the investment in obtaining, verifying and presenting the contents of the database, thereby protecting the investment of money, time or effort that goes into compiling databases

- the exceptions which currently operate in the copyright field relating to research, education and library use continue - except where the Directive specifically requires otherwise (e.g. the limitation of the research exception to non-commercial research)

- similar provisions for remedies, and for the jurisdiction of the Copyright Tribunal, are made for the database right as those which exist for copyright

- the inclusion of an unfair extraction and reutilisation right which provides a 15-year period of protection from completion or publication for the database itself. This 15-year period is renewed whenever there is a substantial change to the database. It can be argued, therefore, that a database which is being continually updated and from which old material is deleted will be perpetually covered by the extraction right

- the definition of a database includes the materials necessary for the operation of the database. This includes the database thesaurus, index, and its means of presentation.

The Department of Trade and Industry set up a Database Market Strategy Group to monitor the impact, including the economic impact, of the new regulations on the education, library and publishing sectors[31]. The membership of the group was announced in November 1998[32]. The members include representatives of both database producers and users. The membership is given below to illustrate the different interests represented, although there may be one or two changes to the list resulting from changes of job (although, at the time of writing I am unaware of any changes of membership of the committee having been formally announced). However, at the time of writing the Database Market Strategy Group had met only once, and there are no plans for a second meeting.

Database Marketing Strategy Group

Toby Bainton, Secretary, Standing Conference of National and University Libraries

Clive Bradley CBE, Director, Confederation of Information Communication Industries

Roger Broadie, Chairman, Copyright and Designs Committee, Trade Marks, Patents and Designs Federation

Professor Roger Elliot FRS, The Royal Society

Trevor Fenwick, Director, Joint Head of Public Affairs, Directory and Databases Publishers Association

Frank Harris, Chair/Convenor, Educational Copyright Users' Forum

Anne Joseph, Legal Director, Reed Elsevier (UK) Ltd

Henry Manisty, Head of Government and Regulatory Affairs, Reuters

Ross Shimmon, former Chief Executive, the Library Association

Steve Sidaway, Sales and Marketing Director, Chadwyck-Healey Ltd

---

The Library Association has produced a set of guidelines which provide a summary of the main provisions affecting libraries and archives. The guidelines outline four scenarios illustrating how database products are likely to be protected, and these are reproduced below[33]:

1.   If the database contents are selected, collected and assembled in an original way, then the database (compilation) has copyright protection for the full 70 year term. If the contents are also original these will also have copyright protection. Examples of this type of database include the *Times newspaper on CD-ROM*, *Chemical Abstracts*, *Library and Information Services Abstracts (LISA)*, and *Encyclopaedia Britannica*.

2.   If the database contents are selected, collected and assembled in an original way, then the database (compilation) has copyright protection for the full 70 year term. If the contents are not original but the maker has invested heavily in its making they will be protected by the database right for 15 years. Examples of this type of database are *Whitaker's Books in Print*, *Yellow Pages* (most of the straightforward listings of names and addresses in *Yellow Pages* are not original).

3.   If the database contents are not selected, collected and assembled in an original way, then the database itself will have no protection. If the contents of this database are not original but the maker has invested heavily in its making, they will be protected by the database

right for 15 years. Examples of this type of database are: white pages telephone directories and other simple A-Z listings such as *The Directory of British Associations* and the *Aslib Directory* (although some of the indexes may qualify for copyright protection), simple TV listings.

4.   If the database contents are not selected, collected and assembled in an original way, then the database itself will have no protection. If the contents of this database are however original these will have copyright protection. Examples of this type of database are: A-Z listings of all companies where each entry contains original information about the company.

5. Licensing of electronic resources

The nature of library and information services has been totally transformed in recent years by technological advances. Information workers are making use of electronic information as a matter of routine. In their daily work they are searching the Internet, accessing externally published materials across intranets, searching CD-ROMs on a network, setting up profiles of their users interests in order to deliver tailored updates of news (a 'Daily Me') or other types of information using push technology and so on.

Taking into account this prolific increase of information available in electronic format, particularly over the Internet, it is of paramount importance for librarians to become more fully aware of what is and what is not permitted by law.

With hard copy books and journals, you are buying the use of those works in perpetuity. This differs from the situation in the electronic environment where librarians often buy access to material for a specific period of time and usage. Access is normally given after a licence has been signed and the licence is regulated by contract law.

The use and copying of works in electronic form poses particular problems for library and information professionals. The legislative framework for copying from books and journals in hard-copy significantly restricts the permitted levels of copying. However, for paper-based materials, information staff have at least been able to set up licences under collective licensing schemes such as those available from the Copyright Licensing Agency and the Newspaper Licensing Agency which have enabled them to undertake greater levels of copying within the terms of those licences than would be allowed by statute law alone. This has meant that they have been able to undertake copying across a range of materials without having to liaise directly with each individual publisher. The CLA and the NLA have only recently started to offer licences which cover electronic information. However the range of publications covered is likely to be narrower than for the copying of printed material in books, journals and newspapers; and in the case of the CLA, licences covering digital information are only currently available for the higher education and the pharmaceutical sectors.

Copyright compliance for electronic information has become something of an administrative headache for librarians. Information workers have had to rely on the contracts and licences for each individual product, and they have had to familiarise themselves with the conditions of each licence agreement held by their organisation in order to ensure licence compliance. This makes it somewhat impractical to enforce terms which may vary with each individual electronic product. Some people would argue along the lines that digital products cannot be sold except by a licence and that if the licence which accompanies the digital product does not meet the licensee's needs, it is open to the licensee to renegotiate at the time of acquisition. This line of thinking continues, saying that licences are contracts and there are two parties to every contract. These licences, which are evolving, define the primary use of the digital material. It is up to both parties to ensure that the contracts meet their needs and expectations. If a library purchases a product which has a shrink-wrap licence or a 'point and click' licence – where you click to accept the terms and conditions as part of the installation process - where does that leave room for negotiation?

Whilst it is true that publishers clearly want to sell their products and that there may be some room for negotiation concerning the contract, I think that the commercial reality is that the bigger organisations who have to pay heftier licence fees will inevitably have more bargaining power. And it also depends upon the negotiating skills of the information professional. In organisations which have in-house lawyers, they need to work very closely with those lawyers to ensure that the contract truly represents the commercial deal that has been negotiated. If librarians have to negotiate licences with each supplier individually, this is a time consuming process. Thankfully, there have been a number of initiatives for producing model licences and some of these are outlined below.

European Copyright User Platform (ECUP)

ECUP has produced a number of site licences for use with electronic publications. There are 4 licences, covering public[34], national[35], university[36], and company[37] libraries. ECUP has produced a useful set of notes on how to avoid the legal pitfalls[38]; they have a number of sample licences, and some licence clauses which are favourable to libraries[39].

International Coalition of Library Consortia (ICOLC)

The ICOLC produced a 'statement of current perspective and preferred practices for the selection and purchase of electronic information'[40] which established an international perspective on consortial licensing and the purchasing of electronic information by libraries.

John Cox Associates

A number of standard licences have been developed for use by publishers, librarians and subscription agents for electronic resources[41]. These were sponsored by and developed in close co-operation with five major subscription agents: Blackwell, Dawson (now RoweCom), EBSCO, Harrassowitz and Swets. Four types of licence have been produced covering single academic institutions, academic consortia, public libraries, and corporate and other special libraries.

Tilburg University Library

Tilburg University library has issued a set of licensing principles. In the preamble to the document, it states that 'cooperation between publishers should be encouraged in order to stimulate optimal dissemination of scientific information in the electronic age and to develop acceptable conditions and arrangements for electronic publishing with long-term application'[42] and consequently they issued a set of licensing principles.

Heron[43]

The Higher Education Resources ON-demand (Heron) project is part of the Electronic Libraries Programme (eLib), established by the Joint Information Systems Committee (JISC) following the recommendations of the Follett Report of 1993 on the use of information technology in university libraries.

Heron is made up of a consortium of the Universities of Stirling, Napier and South Bank, Blackwell's Bookshops and Blackwell's Information Services. Work began on the project in August 1998. Higher Education Institutions are invited to become subscribing members who will be able to request material from the Heron resource bank for clearance and digitisation. Heron will work closely with the CLA and others to ensure that rapid and effective copyright-clearance mechanisms are in place and that rightsholders receive a fair return.

NESLI[44]

The National Electronic Site License Initiative (NESLI) is an initiative to deliver a national electronic journal service to the UK higher education and research community. The Joint Information Systems Committee (JISC) of the Higher Education Funding Councils appointed Swets and Manchester Computing as managing agent of NESLI, and a model site licence has been produced[45]

PA/JISC

A working party of the Joint Information Systems Committee and the Publishers Association produced a model licence between UK universities and publishers. The final version of the licence was issued in January 1999 [46, 47]

Other resources

- Principles for licensing electronic resources July 15, 1997 (AALL, ALA, AAHSL, ARL, MLA, SLA)[48]

- License depot(sm): a web database of electronic journal and licensing issues (Faxon)[49]

- California state university licences to online information resources: user rights and restrictions[50]

- Let there be light! A conference on licensing electronic resources: state of the evolving art San Francisco, December 8-9 1996[51]

- Basic principles for managing intellectual property in the digital environment (National Humanities Alliance March 24, 1997)[52.]

CLA

In January 1998 the CLA announced that representatives of authors and publishers had endorsed in principle their plans to license the digitisation of existing print material[53]. It was not the intention for the licence to cover any electronically published material such as CD-ROMs, multimedia or online publications. Rather, 'the rights licensed will be non-exclusive and restricted to those necessary to produce an exact electronic facsimile of an existing printed page, but permitted versions will include a 'locked' version of Adobe Acrobat's .pdf format, as well as page images such as .bmp and .tiff'[54].

Then in February 1999, the Copyright Licensing Agency launched their digitisation licensing programme[55]. This offers rightsholders the opportunity to opt into the CLA's licensing schemes on a non-exclusive, sector-by-sector basis. The first licences to be offered are for the higher education and the pharmaceutical sectors.

The programme is based upon 4 key principles imposed by groups representing rightsholders

- transaction only (managed and cleared via CLARCS)
- exact page representation
- rightsholders opt-in
- rightsholder-determined fees.

NLA

The Newspaper Licensing Agency made available an electronic extension in early 1998. This is a legal document supplemental to the basic licence from the NLA that permits the electronic distribution of cuttings. It covers the scanning by the licensee of cuttings for in-house use, and the internal distribution via the intranet of those cuttings. Where licence-holders wish to retain the cuttings in an electronic database, an archive extension is available. This is set out in a document entitled *'Electronic distribution of cuttings – guidance notes for NLA licensees'* dated February 1998.

6. UK legislation

The current legislative framework consists of The Copyright, Designs and Patents Act 1988 which came into force on 1 August 1989 supplemented by a number of statutory instruments which have been issued under the Act. (*NB the list of statutory instruments given below is not a comprehensive list of the subsidiary legislation. Rather it is a list of the ones of most relevance to library and information professionals*).

Primary legislation

Copyright, Designs and Patents Act 1988. Chapter 48. London: HMSO, 1988. ISBN 0105448885

Secondary legislation

SI 1989/1212   *The Copyright (Librarians and Archivists) (Copying of Copyright Material) Regulations 1989.* ISBN 0110972120. London: HMSO, 1989.

Came into force on 1 August 1989. The regulations revoke and replace the Copyright (Libraries) Regulations 1957. They prescribe the descriptions of libraries and archives which may, subject to the prescribed conditions, make and supply copies of copyright works to persons for the purposes of research or private study or to other libraries or archives requiring copies of such works for reference purposes or to replace lost or damaged items in their permanent collection where it is not reasonably practicable to purchase the items.

SI 1992/3233 *The Copyright (Computer Programs) Regulations 1992.* ISBN 0110251164 London: HMSO, 1992.

Came into force on 1 January 1993 implementing directive 91/250/EEC on the legal protection of computer programs.

SI 1995/3297 *Copyright Rights in Performances: the Duration of Copyright and Rights in Performances Regulations 1995.* ISBN 011 0538331 London: HMSO, 1995.

Came into force on 1 January 1996 implementing directive 93/98/EEC harmonizing the term of protection of copyright and certain related rights. The duration of copyright was increased from 50 years to 70 years.

SI 1996/2967 *Copyright and Related Rights Regulations 1996.* ISBN 0110633342 London: HMSO, 1996.

Came into force on 1st December 1996 implementing directive 92/100/EEC on rental right and lending right and certain rights related to copyright in the field of intellectual property ('the Rental Directive') and of directive 93/83/EEC on the co-ordination of certain rules concerning copyright and rights related to copyright applicable to satellite broadcasting and cable re-transmission ('the Satellite and Cable Directive'). They also implement certain provisions of Council Directive 93/98/EEC harmonising the term of protection of copyright and certain related rights.

SI 1997/3032   *The Copyright and Rights in Databases Regulations 1997.* ISBN 0110653254. London: The Stationery Office, 1998.

Came into force on 1 January 1998 implementing directive 96/9/EC. This harmonises the laws of EU member states on copyright in databases, and introduced a new form of protection for some databases. s29 of the CDPA 1988 is amended to comply with the EC directive that copying from databases should be for non-commercial purposes only. Previously, UK law had not distinguished between academic, scientific or commercial research.

7. EU documents

Directives

Council directive **91/250/EEC** of 14 May 1991 on the legal protection of computer programs L122/42 [implemented in the UK by SI 1992/3233]

Council directive **92/100/EEC** of 19 November 1992 on rental right and lending right and on certain rights relating to copyright in the field of intellectual property OJ 1992 L346/61 [implemented in the UK by SI 1996/2967]

Council directive **93/98/EEC** of 29 October 1993 harmonizing the term of protection of copyright and certain related rights OJ 1993 L290/9 [implemented in the UK by SI 1995/3297]

Council directive **96/9/EC** of the European Parliament and of the council of 11 March 1996 on the legal protection of databases OJ 1996 L77/20 27 March 1996 [implemented in the UK by SI 1997/3032]

Proposals

Green paper on copyright and the challenge of technology **COM(88) 172** final

Communication from the Commission to the Council and the European Parliament, to the Economic and Social Committee and to the Committee of the

Regions, Europe's way to the information society: an action plan (**COM(94) 347** final)

Green paper on copyright and related rights in the information society **COM(95) 382** final 19 July 1995

Proposal for a Council Decision approving the Council of Europe Convention relating to copyright and neighbouring rights in the framework of transborder broadcasting by satellite **COM(96)6** OJ 1996 C164/3

Follow-up to the green paper on copyright and related rights in the information society. 21 November 1996. **COM(96) 568** final

Proposal for a European Parliament and Council Directive on the harmonization of certain aspects of copyright and related rights in the Information Society. Proposal adopted by Commission 10 December 1997. **COM(97) 628** final OJ 1998 C108/6 21 January 1998

Proposal for a council decision on the approval, on behalf of the European Community, of the WIPO Copyright Treaty and the WIPO Performances and Phonograms Treaty **COM(1998) 249** final OJ C165/ 8 27 April 1998

Amended proposal for a European parliament and council directive on the harmonisation of certain aspects of copyright and related rights in the information society. **COM(1999) 250 final**, 21st May 1999

Press Releases

IP/95/798 Green paper on copyright and related rights in the information society

IP/96/1042 Communication on copyright and related rights in the information society

IP/96/171 Legal protection of databases directive adopted

IP/97/1100 Proposal for a directive on copyright and related rights in the information society

Memo/97/108   Background to the proposal for directive on copyright and related rights in the information society

IP/99/377 Amended proposal for directive on copyright and related rights in the information society

Other items

Europe and the global information society: Recommendations of the high-level group on the information society to the Corfu European Council. (known as the Bangemann report). Bulletin of the European Union Supplement 2/94 pp6-39.

8. International treaties and conventions

Berne Copyright Convention (Berne Convention for the Protection of Literary and Artistic Works Paris Act of July 24, 1971 (as amended on September 28, 1979)

The Berne Convention is one of the major international agreements on copyright. The first agreement was signed in 1886, but the most recent revision took place in Paris in 1971.

Universal Copyright Convention

A UNESCO conference in 1952 held in Geneva led to the adoption of the Universal Copyright Convention (UCC).

Trade-Related Aspects of Intellectual Property Rights (TRIPS) element of the World Trade Agreement[56]

A major part of the GATT text which was agreed in 1993. This agreement is designed to ensure that IP rights do not themselves become barriers to legitimate trade.

WIPO copyright treaty 1996[57]

WIPO is a United Nations body which is responsible for administering many of the international conventions on intellectual property. It is not only concerned with copyright, but also administers international agreements on patents, trademarks and other aspects of intellectual property.

On 20 December 1996, two Treaties on the protection of authors ('WIPO Copyright Treaty') and on the protection of performers and phonogram producers ('WIPO Performances and Phonograms Treaty') were adopted by about one hundred countries who are members of WIPO, the World Intellectual Property Organisation.

The European Commission issued a press release about the two new treaties on 16 January 1997 (IP/ 96/1244 'WIPO Diplomatic Conference concludes its work: two new Treaties on intellectual property adopted in Geneva on 20 December 1996').

The WIPO copyright treaty complements the Berne Convention for the Protection of Literary and Artistic Works, which was last revised in 1971 and adapts it to the digital environment.

At the WIPO meeting in December 1996, however, a decision on the controversial Database Treaty was postponed.

Reports from the meeting and discussion are given as postings to the ECUP (European Copyright User Platform) discussion list. The archive to this list can be found at http:// www.kaapeli.fi/hypermail/ ecup-list/ (accessed 13.3.2000.)

The text of the treaty is accessible on the WIPO web site at http:// www.wipo.org/eng/diplconf/ distrib/94dc.htm (accessed 13.3.2000.)

9. Case law

The prospect of organisations which infringe copyright being faced with legal action resulting in substantial costs and damages or even criminal prosecution is a powerful weapon in convincing those organisations not to undertake illegal photocopying in the workplace.

Licensing bodies such as the Copyright Licensing Agency and the Newspaper Licensing Agency are prepared to institute legal proceedings, if necessary, in order to enforce the rights entrusted to them by authors and publishers. The CLA's Copywatch campaign, for example, uses the latest investigative techniques – including employing undercover detectives – to expose copyright theft in local and national government, schools and colleges, as well as business. The anti-copyright theft campaign has a hotline which was set up for those who have confidential information about illegal copying as well as for companies that wish to take out a licence.

The press coverage which follows successful actions is highly embarrassing for the infringers, and often leads businesses and institutions to check that they are complying with copyright law.

The chapter heading of 'case law' is something of a misnomer, because many of the cases either never went to court, or else they were settled out of court and consequently they are unreported and uncited. So, a number of the 'cases' outlined below were legal actions rather than court cases.

Publishers Association v Manchester City Council (1984)

In 1984 the Publishers Association took a representative action on behalf of two publishers and two authors and all its other members following the discovery of hundreds of photocopies of a standard mathematics textbook. The author of the book was a supply teacher. One day he was sent to a school in Manchester where on opening a cupboard to get the textbooks for the lesson he was surprised when quantities of photocopies of his own book fell about his feet. Manchester City Council was ordered to pay £75,000 for the copyright infringement. The costs and publicity resulting from that case persuaded local authorities to sign up for a schools licence with the CLA.

'Copyright – behaving properly' Elizabeth Bramwell [Licensing Manager, CLA] IN *The Law Librarian* vol 28 no 1 March 1997 pp15-17

Copyright Licensing Agency v Morgan Stanley (1991)

An overenthusiastic individual at Morgan Stanley copied a £75 book on 'Warrants, options and convertibles' and then distributed one photocopy to a client and kept 22 for internal use. This infringement by the person deeply embarrassed Morgan Stanley when it found out what had happened.

'Copyright – behaving properly' Elizabeth Bramwell [Licensing Manager, CLA] IN *The Law Librarian* vol 28 no 1 March 1997 pp15-17

Copyright Licensing Agency v Essenheath t/a Greenwich College (1994)

The CLA, acting on behalf of publishers, the Open University and Centaur Press, obtained a considerable financial settlement for unauthorized photocopying from Essenheath Ltd, the trading arm of Greenwich College, an independent business college in London. The CLA hired a private investigator to enrol as a student and found evidence that the college had reproduced copyright material without permission or licence for use in course work by students. The college was ordered to take out a CLA licence.

Copyright in industrial and commercial libraries 4th ed. by Sandy Norman p62.

Copyright Licensing Agency v Fournier Pharmaceuticals Ltd (1995)

Fournier Pharmaceuticals Ltd is the British affiliate of the leading French pharmaceutical company, Groupe Fournier, which is one of the largest private companies in France. The company accepted that copyright had been infringed in an internal current awareness bulletin circulated to its sales and marketing staff. Publications that were cited included articles from the British Medical Journal and the Lancet. Fournier Pharmaceuticals Ltd reached an out of court settlement for copyright infringements, and agreed to take out a Business Photocopying Licence with the CLA.

CLA news release April 1995

Copyright Licensing Agency v Store Street Press (1996)

Undercover detectives acting on CLA's behalf, investigated the Store Street Press copyshop, after CLA received reports of an operation to cheat authors and publishers. CLA's investigators found huge quantities of photocopying being undertaken by the shop without either a CLA licence or the authorisation of the publishers. The offending copying mainly comprised course packs (including large excerpts from works published by Cambridge University Press, Elsevier, Macmillan, Penguin and Routledge) for students at the School of Oriental and African Studies (a college of London University).

Copying on the scale discovered would leave owners and managers of copyshops open to a criminal prosecution as well as the substantial damages and costs. All universities have CLA licences and are able to produce course packs upon payment of an additional fee to the CLA.

The Copyright Licensing Agency exposed and stopped this photocopying scam.

CLA news release 4th November 1996

Copyright Licensing Agency v Dar Al Handasah (1996)

The CLA took Dar Al Handasah, one of the largest structural engineering consultancies in the UK, to the High Court claiming for extensive copyright infringement over a long period of time. Dar Al Handasah Consultants (UK) Limited settled with the Copyright Licensing Agency and four of its mandating publishers for a sum of £50,000 in damages and costs. Dar Al Handasah also agreed to take out a CLA licence.

The action was made possible as a result of a whistleblower who rang the CLA's Copywatch hotline. CLA then took steps to confirm the accuracy of the accusations by employing a firm of private investigators to obtain evidence.

CLA news release 2nd December, 1996

American Geophysical Union v Texaco Inc. 12 USPQ 2d 1545 (2d Cir. 1994)

Even though there are differences between US and UK copyright law, this was a landmark case which was seen as adding strength to the CLA's efforts to get companies to take out a copyright licence with them.

In October 1994, over 80 publishers of scientific and technical journals brought a case against Texaco claiming that the copying by its scientists and engineers of articles from the journals for future reference constituted copyright infringement. In order to simplify the litigation, the case was limited to the specific issue of whether the copying was 'fair use' under US copyright legislation on facts which were limited to copying of eight specific articles by one chemical engineer. Each of the journals in question included general statements that no parts of the journal could be copied without the permission of the copyright owner. It appears that it was general practice for the library at Texaco to circulate the journals and for researchers to make personal copies of any articles which they considered useful to keep for future reference.

The decision of the court was based on the facts before them, and it was made clear that this was not a broad ruling that photocopying for research purposes could never be fair. Nevertheless the court did take account of the existence of a collective licensing scheme by the Copyright Clearance Center as well as the existence of document delivery services and contrasted this with Texaco's 'free' archival copying by researchers which they felt was prejudicial to rightsholders.

Her Majesty's Stationery Office v Compliance Ltd and Reed Elsevier (UK) Ltd (trading as Butterworths) (1995)

Her Majesty's Stationery Office, which administers crown copyright, issued writs and began a legal action against Compliance which produced the manuals on CD-ROM in a joint venture with Butterworths. The writs claimed infringement of crown copyright and sought an injunction to restrict further publication. In 1994 the Inland Revenue brought the manuals into the public domain through a contract with Tolley Publishing. Both the Inland Revenue and Tolley had understood the contract to be on an exclusive basis.

The case was settled out of court. Subsequently Tolley became part of the Reed group, of which Butterworths is also a part. On 9 February 1996 Roger Freeman, the then minister for public service, said that the government would continue its existing policy of allowing secondary publishers, without charge or prior permission and on a non-exclusive basis, to reproduce in value-added print format Acts, statutory instruments and statutory rules and orders. But, more importantly, Mr Freeman announced that this concession would now be extended to electronic and microform formats[58].

On 29 October 1996 Roger Freeman announced a new and simplified set of crown copyright licensing arrangements to make it easier for electronic publishers to include official material in their information services. The copyright licence, QLM/3[59], which is renewable after seven years, means that publishers will be able to reproduce quasi-legislative material without making prior permission from the Crown at a standardised royalty rate. This type of information includes codes of practice and official guidance for administrators on the interpretation of statute[60].

Shetland Times Ltd v Dr. Jonathan Wills and Zetnews Ltd (1996) (commonly referred to as Shetland Times v Shetland News)

The weekly Shetland Times newspaper sought a permanent ban on certain kinds of unsolicited hypertext links from the Shetland News, a daily Internet news magazine. The Shetland News reproduced verbatim a number of headlines appearing in The Shetland Times. These headlines were hyperlinked to the Shetland News web site. Clicking on the headline took the reader directly to the internal pages on the Shetland Times site on which the related story was found. The court stated that 'access to the pursuer's [Shetland Times] items ... can be obtained by by-passing the pursuers' front page and accordingly missing any advertising material which may appear on it'[61]

The case was settled out of court on 11th November 1997, with each side paying its own legal costs. The Shetland News agreed that links to stories from the Shetland Times would in future only be made under the following conditions:

(a)   that each link to any individual story would be acknowledged by the legend 'A Shetland Times Story' appearing underneath each headline of the same or similar size as the headline

(b)   adjacent to any such headline(s) there shall appear a button showing legibly the Shetland Times masthead logo; and

(c)   the legend and the button shall each be hypertext links to the Shetland Times online headline page.

Because the case was settled out of court, we will have to wait for a legal precedent to be set on this issue in the UK.

Newspaper Licensing Agency v Islington Borough Council (1998)

The Newspaper Licensing Agency granted a licence to Islington Borough Council but the council refused to pay the NLA's invoice. When it proved impossible to resolve the matter out of court, the Newspaper Licensing Agency brought a civil action for copyright infringement. The council accepted an undertaking that it would not copy cuttings from newspapers in the NLA's repertoire unless licensed to do so.

Council pay for copyright breach. *NLA press release* http://www.nla.co.uk/welcome/htm/isl.htm (accessed 13.3.2000)

Newspaper Licensing Agency v Marks and Spencer PLC (1999)

The copying by Marks & Spencer plc of newspaper articles without a licence from the Newspaper Licensing Agency was held to be a clear breach of copyright.

Judge holds copying by Marks and Spencer unlawful. NLA press release (http://www.nla.co.uk/welcome/htm/m&s.htm) (accessed 13.3.2000).

There have been a number of instances where, although it didn't come to the issue of proceedings, damages have been paid to the NLA by companies and others for their admitted infringement. These include: British United Provident Association (BUPA), Conservative Central Office, The Labour Party, The Liberal Democrats, and Pilkington plc.

Source: http//www.nla.co.uk/welcome/htm/lawnotes.htm (accessed 13.3.2000).

Copyright Tribunal cases

In the past few years the Newspaper Licensing Agency has had a number of legal actions before the Copyright Tribunal, which include:

The Institute of Public Relations v the Newspaper Licensing Agency Ltd (CDPA s119 CT53/97)

The Public Relations Consultants Association Ltd v the Newspaper Licensing Agency Ltd (CDPA s119 CT 56/97)

Romeike and Curtice Ltd v Newspaper Licensing Agency Ltd (CDPA s125 CT 47/97)

The Patent Office web site maintains information on both applications/references currently before the Copyright Tribunal (http://www.patent.gov.uk/dpolicy/ctapps.html, accessed 13.3.2000) and decisions and orders issued by the Copyright Tribunal (http://www.patent.gov.uk/dpolicy/ctdecis.html) (accessed 13.3.2000).

10. Copyright in the work environment

This publication is intended to be a short guide to copyright from the point of view of library and information professionals, and as such I felt that it would be helpful to find out from several library managers how they deal with copyright matters. The library managers of three libraries in commercial organisations were interviewed to find out the kind of practical questions that they have to tackle in their day to day work. The case studies are followed by a series of questions and answers, using questions which information practitioners have asked.

Case study 1 (Consulting engineers)

This firm of consulting engineers has a copyright licence with the Newspaper Licensing Agency. The Library and Information Services Manager made a point of saying that they had found the NLA to be fair, reasonable, and easy to deal with; a view which contrasts strongly with their impression of the CLA. They were, however, unaware of the NLA's electronic extension to the main licence; or to the fact that it was now possible to pay a licence fee to the NLA to cover a number of US newspapers. For electronic access to newspapers, the library uses Reuters Business Briefing whose subscription costs already take account of copyright royalties; but they may wish to look at scanning cuttings onto their intranet at some point in the future.

The firm uses the BSI's 'Barbour Construction Expert' which has got the main standards on it. The product is networked to the engineers, and it gives the library a visible presence within the firm. If the standard is not on Barbour Construction Expert, then they work closely with Barbour to get the standard onto the product. The licence agreement allows users to retain printouts of standards for no more than 30 days. Engineers are told not to retain out of date documents.

The library manager mentioned that another department dealt with Ordnance Survey material, and that they had a CD-ROM product where you paid for each item retrieved, and they believed that the fee included a copyright royalty.

The librarian had a negative impression of the Copyright Licensing Agency, seeing it as an unaccountable quango. They felt that the CLA's approach was both rude and hostile. The library manager mentioned that the CLA had been targetting engineering companies, but that when they had looked at the CLA licence they found that the key publishers that they deal with such as BSI were excluded from the CLA's licence. The librarian did speak to the firm's legal department about the CLA licence, and it was decided not to take out a licence. Instead, a notice was issued by the legal department which outlined what people can and cannot do. The library does not have any copyright posters displayed such as those from Aslib or the Library Association.

In order to keep up to date with copyright issues, the librarian reads the Institute of Information Scientists's *Journal of Information Science*, particularly the LISLEX section covering legal issues in library and information science and IIS Inform. They also read Managing Information and the Library Association Record.Whilst they do try to make time to do some professional reading, they don't get time to look at the websites of organisations such as the Patent Office or the Copyright Licensing Agency. The librarian said that it was a full time job keeping up with copyright issues.

The Library & Information Services Manager feels that copyright is certainly an issue, indeed a 'permanent cloud'. It was felt that publishers' can't get their act together, especially in a climate where we are all moving to information being available in electronic format. Having said that, the library manager had not been following the CLA's digitisation licensing programme initiative, and was unaware of the NLA's electronic extension to the main licence. It was also felt that there should be more transparency concerning the cost of the licences.

Members of the library team attend training courses which cover copyright as an element within them. These courses could be from organisations such as TFPL, or they may be free seminars. Jeremy Phillips and Charles Oppenheim were seen as key copyright experts, and if an article had been written by either of these people or a seminar was being presented by them they would make a point of attending such a seminar or reading such an article.

The library manager is seen as the contact for enquiries about copyright. The library deals with questions such as 'Can I copy this British Standard?'. They also have situations where engineers want a number of references which are all from the same journal, and they have to explain to the user that this is not permitted.

Case study 2 (Law firm)

The second case study was a medium-sized law firm based in the city of London. The firm had copyright licences in place from a number of licensing bodies - the Copyright Licensing Agency, the Newspaper Licensing Agency and also with Ordnance Survey. The Library Manager perceived copyright to be more of an issue now by comparison with a couple of years ago, and she identified a number of reasons why this should be the case. The Newspaper Licensing Agency had only been set up in 1996 and the Copyright Licensing Agency had only recently started to target law firms. Usage of the Internet had in that time also become an integral part of providing library services, and this was raising a number of issues. For example, the Times Law Reports are available on the web, but the Library Manager at this law firm would ideally like to be able to download the law reports from the web and distribute them to interested fee-earners within the firm.

The Library Manager said that library users had asked her a number of questions about copyright. These included:

- Can I send a photocopy of this item to client X?

- Is it alright to photocopy handed down judgment Y and give it to a publisher?

- Is it permitted to make multiple copies of Stationery Office publication Z to hand out at a seminar?

She had also contacted information providers on a number of occasions in order to check up on the copyright position for particular situations.

The Library Manager said that we as library and information professionals have a role to play in delivering information and that the need for information is very strong. In order to achieve this she said that we need the copyright regime to be practical and realistic. She recognised that there was a need for librarians to lobby in order to achieve this; but felt that day-to-day pressures of work make it very difficult for information professionals to find the time to do any lobbying. She did consider that we ought to get lawyers involved on our side, mentioning an issue of *European Intellectual Property Review* in which lawyers had written about the copyright problems faced by librarians; and thought that this might be achieved by contacting an intellectual property grouping of lawyers and/or the City of London Law Society team who negotiated the law firm licence with the CLA.

The library did not have a big journal stock, but was inundated with requests for journal articles as a result of sending out a regular current awareness bulletin which included details of articles which were not held in-house. Document supply services were used to satisfy these requests, and users were informed of the costs of obtaining the items which had been requested. The Library Manager also sometimes needed to tell library users that certain items could not be copied by the document supply service because of the policy of the publisher.

Law firms have access to a union list of the journals and law reports held by participating firms. This list is maintained by the City Law Librarians Group. However, the Library Manager commented that in the light of copyright practices coming under much closer scrutiny, information staff were much more cautious. She knew of at least one firm who had refused to participate in the union list because of concerns over copyright.

The Library Manager said that she felt there was a need for a guide to best practice in copyright procedures, so that she could use it as something to work towards. She also felt that there was a need for a clear and concise practical guide for librarians on the implementation of copyright legislation.

Case study 3 (Engineering firm)

The third case study was an engineering firm. The firm has in place licences from the Copyright Licensing Agency and Ordnance Survey. The organisation also has a CD-ROM of British Standards where they have a licence agreement under which printouts from the CD-ROM are only to be kept for a maximum of 30 days, and where a tally is kept of items printed out. This is then sent off to BSI, who charge the firm annually for the level of usage at a rate of 44p per page. At present, the company does not have a licence with the Newspaper Licensing Agency, but the Library Manager thinks that they will probably get one. The firm relies on online services instead of providing a press clippings service, and they also buy multiple copies of the daily newspapers.

The Library Manager did not feel that copyright was any more of an issue than it was two years ago. She did, however, feel that library users need to be more aware of what is permitted. They have copyright posters, and notices on the photocopying machines. The organisation's staff handbook also had a section about copyright. Library users do regularly ask library staff for advice on copyright.

In order to keep up to date with copyright issues, the Library Manager relied on reading the professional press; especially anything written by Graham Cornish, Charles Oppenheim, or Sandy Norman and also upon personal contacts. The staff library contains a number of books on copyright, and the whole area of copyright is discussed at library staff meetings.

Some library staff are unsure of the legal position on a number of points such as whether you can make more than one copy of the same article from a journal or make a copy of more than one article from the same journal. In order to overcome this uncertainty, the Library Manager had arranged for a copyright expert to come in chat to them at their library staff meeting.

One point which the Library Manager made was that she felt that the librarians were sometimes seen as an obstruction, and that they are put in a difficult position between library users and rights owners. She felt that it was therefore very important to be sure of what you are saying, and that library staff needed proper training. She thought that the law was vague on a number of points, and that even when you speak to experts in the field, they can only come up with a reply such as 'well, possibly', and that in some ways you had to rely on a best guess. The Library Manager felt that it was up to individual librarians to do what they could to overcome these difficulties, and that it is part of one's professionalism.

There have been instances when the Library Manager has checked points on copyright with the information providers, and in some cases has found that they themselves have been unable to give clear answers on what is permitted. The Library Manager felt that copyright was something which is almost impossible to police, and that there needs to be some way of controlling it. She thought that it was difficult to get people to take it seriously, and when questioned about this it was clear that she was referring both to library users and to librarians generally. When people are told that they could be prosecuted for infringing behaviour, they grin and see it as a joke. They do not perceive it to be a huge danger. She also felt that amongst our professional colleagues, copyright is not seen to be inspiring. It is not considered to be one of the most interesting topics, rather it is seen as being something rather boring.

I asked the Library Manager what she would say to someone coming new into the profession wanting to know more about copyright. The answer was that the person should read the professional press, go to meetings, join a professional group, but also to be willing to call up people like the CLA to see if they could go and have a general chat to clarify a number of points concerning the current copyright regime.

Questions asked by information practitioners

(i) How do you enforce copyright law where public access to photocopiers is concerned?

Whilst librarians are not the rights owners and it is not really their job to challenge people, it is also not their job to encourage copyright infringement. I would therefore recommend that you do whatever you can to ensure copyright compliance such as putting up posters next to photocopiers which outline what the recommended limits are, and also putting notices on the copying machines themselves.

(ii) Are blanket bans on reproduction of material by copyright holders legal?

Some publishers do put notices on their publications claiming that copying any part of the publication is not permitted. I would say that the statutory exceptions (fair dealing and library privilege) do still apply, and that this type of notice can therefore be ignored so long as the copying falls within what is permitted by the fair dealing or library privilege exceptions. I understand that in a few instances, the Library Association has challenged publishers who have included such notices in their publications. I would, however, recommend that proper acknowledgement is given of where the information has come from.

(iii) What is the copyright position regarding the downloading of information such as references or abstracts from online databases, and possibly incorporating these into an internal database?

This type of activity is governed by and subject to the terms of the contract with the information provider. If it is not included in your original contract, then you will need to negotiate an acceptable arrangement with the database provider. Dialog, for example, has a system called ERA - electronic redistribution and archiving under which this type of activity is allowed, so long as a special copyright royalty is paid as part of the fee for using the ERA service.

(iv) How do we educate our users in non-abuse etc of the copyright system? Our users think that by signing a form they are absolved from all further responsibility.

It is necessary for library and information staff to raise awareness about copyright. For example, in a commercial organisation this could be done by including a statement in the staff handbook, putting a reminder in the staff newsletter, or placing copyright posters next to all the photocopiers within the firm. Librarians should respect copyright, it is part of being a professional.

(v) What if the author's permission has been obtained, but the publisher's has not. Can an item be copied?

To photocopy beyond the recommended limits, you do need the publisher's permission in order to make the copy, since there is copyright in the typographical arrangement. One way round this would be to get the author to send you a copy of their draft of the item, as that would overcome the problem of getting copyright in the typographical arrangement of the work.

(vi) How should a record of photocopying be kept?

Photocopying under library privilege requires that a copyright declaration form is completed by the library user. The form should be in the format specified in the Copyright (Librarians and Archivists) (Copying of Copyright Material) Regulations 1989

SI 1989/1212. The forms should be retained for a total of seven years (six years plus the current year).

Some librarians have chosen to introduce copyright declaration forms, even where they are not in libraries that fall within the definition of 'prescribed library' as outlined in the 1989 regulations, and they have chosen to do so because of concerns over whether their users are infringing copyright.

(vii) Should 'old' photocopies in subject files all be thrown away?

Sections 41 and 42 of the CDPA 1988 say that so long as the necessary steps are followed, prescribed libraries are able to provide other prescribed libraries with copies of periodical articles, and also to replace items which have been lost, destroyed or damaged. But only prescribed libraries may request and receive photocopies to add to their collections, and this therefore excludes commercial organisations.

Even if you only keep photocopies of articles from journals for which you hold the originals in your library, the problem with keeping such photocopies on file is that library users will want to make a copy from the photocopy rather than the original for the sake of convenience. Unless you have a licence which allows the copying of photocopies [and this is not a part of the standard CLA licence], you would be well advised to avoid keeping photocopies of articles on subject files accessible to library users.

(viii) What if two individuals ask for a copy of the same paper to be ordered from the British Library Document Supply Centre (BLDSC)?

The BLDSC has a licence with the CLA which allows it to make copies beyond the limits of the provisions for libraries in exchange for the payment of royalties as set by the copyright owners. So, it is alright to request more than one copy of the same paper, so long as the royalties have been paid. Librarians should *not* simply photocopy the paper for the second person who requested it.

11. References and notes

1. *Berne Convention for the Protection of Literary and Artistic Works* Paris Act of July 24, 1971, as amended on September 28, 1979 Art 9.2

2. 1883 *Autobiography* ch.12.

3. For a complete list of libraries covered by 'library privilege' see schedule 1 of SI 1989/1212: The Copyright (Librarians and Archivists) (Copying of Copyright Material) Regulations 1989.

4. *The Library Association Code of Professional Conduct and guidance notes.* 1st ed. 1996.

5. Major crackdown on illegal copying launched. CLA news release, 5 December 1996.

6. Whistle blower leads to £50,000 court settlement for the Copyright Licensing Agency. *CLA news release,* 2 December 1996.

7. Hubbard v. Vosper (1972) 2 QB 84

8. http://www.cla.co.uk/www/fairdeal.htm (accessed 13.3.2000).

9. As inserted by regulation 8 of the *Copyright and Rights in Databases Regulations 1997* (SI 1997/ 3032)

10. *Photocopying from books and journals: a guide for all users of copyright literary works* / Charles Clark. British Copyright Council, 1990. ISBN 0901737062. 13pp

11. *Copyright in industrial and commercial libraries* by Sandy Norman. 4th ed. Library Association. p51

12. Copyright - behaving properly by Elizabeth Bramwell IN *The Law Librarian* vol 28 no 1, March 1997 p. 16.

13. 'Major crackdown on illegal copying launched'. *CLA news release* 5 December 1996

14. Copyright clearance service reaches £1 million. CLA news release, 9 April 1999

15. Copyright - behaving properly by Elizabeth Bramwell IN *The Law Librarian*, vol. 28 no. 1, March 1997 p. 15.

16. The CLA has now introduced a digitisation licensing programme, but as yet this covers only higher education and the pharmaceutical sector.

17. The current edition of *Photocopying from newspapers - your guide to the rules* by the Newspaper Licensing Agency is known as 'Copying newspaper cuttings – a general guide to the rules', produced in June 1999.

18. *Copying newspaper cuttings – a general guide to the rules*, 7th ed. June 1999 p2.

19. http://www.patent.gov.uk/dpolicy/abttrib.html (accessed 13.3.2000) 'About the Copyright Tribunal'.

20. *Photocopying of crown and parliamentary copyright material*, HMSO Copyright Unit, 23 September 1996. CO(P) 48/1022. (The 'Dear Librarian' letter)

21. *Crown copyright in the information age: a consultation document on access to public sector information.* Cm 3819. The Stationery Office, 1998. £9.75 ISBN 0101381921. See also Cabinet Office press release CAB 11/98 'Plans to modernise crown copyright announced by David Clark' of 19th January 1998

22. Lord Lester of Herne Hill asked a question on parliamentary copyright. The written answer appears in *House of Lords Parliamentary Debates (Hansard)* 12th January 1998, WA 135 68

23. The future management of crown copyright. Cm 4300. ISBN 0101430027. £9.50. http//www.hmso.gov.uk/document/copywp.htm (accessed 13.3.2000). See also Cabinet Office press release CAB 62/99 of 26 March 1999 Plans to streamline management of crown copyright announced by Jack Cunningham

24. http://www.hmso.gov.uk/guides.htm (accessed 13.3.2000)

25. http://www.inforoute.hmso.gov.uk/inforoute/about.htm (accessed 13.3.2000)

26. *Copyright in industrial and commercial libraries* by Sandy Norman. Library Association, 1999. 4th ed. ISBN 185604324X. 80pp. Library Association Copyright Guidelines. (There are a number of other guides in the same series covering other library sectors).

27. *Copyright: interpreting the law for libraries, archives and information services* by Graham P. Cornish. 3rd ed. Library Association Publishing, 1999. 188pp. ISBN 1856043444

28. 'Whose line is it anyway' by Anthony Julius IN *The Guardian*, Tuesday 10 March 1998 p. 17.

29. 'CLA, copyright and the internet' http://www.cla.co.uk/www/internet.htm (accessed 13.3.2000)

30. Carol Risher's presentation is available as a PDF file from the web site www.doi.org/tech-demo/tech-forum.html (accessed 13.3.2000)

31. 'Ian McCartney announces Database Market Strategy Group' *DTI Press Notice* P/97/805, 3 December 1997.

32. Howells announces membership of the Database Market Strategy Group DTI press notice P/98/901, 16 November 1998

33. The four scenarios are reproduced from *The Copyright and Rights in Databases Regulations 1997: summary of the main provisions affecting libraries and archives*, London, Library Association, 1998. 4pp. Library Association Guidelines

34. http://www.eblida.org/ecup/docs/heads/publib.htm/ (accessed 13.3.2000)

35. http://www.eblida.org/ecup/docs/heads/natlib.htm/ (accessed 13.3.2000)

36. http://www.eblida.org/ecup/docs/heads.unilib.htm/ (accessed 13.3.2000)

37. http://www.eblida.org/ecup/docs/heads/company.htm/ (accessed 13.3.2000)

38. http://www.eblida.org/ecup/docs/1998/warning.htm (accessed 13.3.2000)

39. http://www.eblida.org/ecup/licensing/ (accessed 13.3.2000)

40. http://www.library.yale.edu/consortia/ statement.html (accessed 13.3.2000)

41. http://www.licensingmodels.com (accessed 13.3.2000)

42. http://webdoc.sub.gwdg.de/ebook/aw/ prinzliz/l-lizp-e.htm (accessed 13.3.2000)

43. http://www.stir.ac.uk/infoserv/heron (accessed 13.3.2000)

44. http://www.nesli.ac.uk (accessed 13.3.2000)

45. http://www.nesli.ac.uk/nesli8a.html (accessed 13.3.2000)

46. http://www.ukoln.ac.uk/services/elib/papers/pa/intro.html (accessed 13.3.2000)

47. http://www.ukoln.ac.uk/services/elib/papers/pa/licence/Pajisc21.html (accessed 13.3.2000)

48. http://arl.cni.org.scomm/licensing/ principles.html (accessed 13.3.2000)

49. http://www.faxon.com/html/ind_lr.html (accessed 13.3.2000)

50. http://www.co.calstate.edu/irt/seir/URR/ info.resources.urr.html (accessed 13.3.2000)

51. http://arl.cni.org/scomm/licensing/sum.html (accessed 13.3.2000)

52. http://www-ninch.cni.org/ISSUES/COPYRIGHT/ PRINCIPLES/NHA_Complete.html (accessed 13.3.2000)

53. Rightsholders support CLA moves to licence digitisation. *CLA news release* 23 January 1998.

54. Op cit

55. Copyright licensing agency launches licensing scheme for digitisation. *CLA news release* 26 February 1999.

56. Agreement establishing the World Trade Organisation agreement on Trade-Related Aspects of Intellectual Property Rights. Cm 3046. Treaty Series No. 10 (1996). GATT. HMSO, 1996. £5.50. ISBN 0101304625.

57. World Intellectual Property Organization (WIPO) Copyright Treaty. [Geneva, 2 December 1996 to 20 December 1996]. Cm 3736. The Stationery Office, 1997. £2.00 ISBN 0101373627

58. Roger Freeman announces government plans for crown copyright. Cabinet Office. *Office of Public Service news release* OPS 13/96 of 9 February 1996

59. *Notice to publishers. Reproduction of crown copyright quasi-legislative material in electronic and micrographic form.* Her Majesty's Stationery Office, 1996. (http://www.hmso.gov.uk/qlm3.htm, accessed 13.3.2000)

60. *Government announces new user-friendly crown copyright licence for electronic publishing sector.* Cabinet Office. Office of Public Service news release OPS 157/96 of 29 October 1996

61. *IT + Communications Newsletter*, February 1998 pp29-32

12. Useful books and journals

Brett, Hugh (editor) *European Intellectual Property Review*. Sweet & Maxwell. 12 issues per year. ISSN 01420461.

CLArion: the newsletter of the Copyright Licensing Agency. ISSN 0951-3701

Clark, Charles. *Photocopying from books and journals: a guide for all users of copyright literary works*, London, British Copyright Council, 1990. ISBN 0901 737 062. 13pp.

Cornish, Graham P. *Copyright: interpreting the law for libraries, archives and information services*. 3rd ed., London, Library Association Publishing, 1999. ISBN 1856043444. 188pp.

European Council for Information Associations. *Statement on intellectual property and copyright*, 1996. http://www.aslib.com/ecia/statement.html (accessed 13.3.2000)

Joint Information Systems Committee. *Report of the Joint Information Systems Committee & Publishers Associations Working Party on Fair Dealing in an Electronic Environment*. Joint Information Systems Committee. July 1997. 17pp.

Library Association. *The Copyright and Rights in Databases Regulations 1997: summary of the main provisions affecting libraries and archives*, London, Library Association, 1998. 4pp. Library Association Guidelines

Newspaper Licensing Agency. *Copying from newspaper cuttings – a general guide to the rules*, Tunbridge Wells, Newspaper Licensing Agency, 7th edition, June 1999.

Norman, Sandy. *Copyright in industrial and commercial libraries*, 4th ed., London, Library Association Publishing, 1999. ISBN 185604324X [Library Association Copyright Guides]. 80pp.

Phillips, Jeremy (editor). *Aslib guide to copyright*, London, Aslib, 1994. Looseleaf. ISBN 0851423116

UNESCO. *Copyright Bulletin*. UNESCO Publishing (further information is available at: http://www.unesco.org/general/eng/publish/period.html (accessed 13.3.2000)

Wall, Raymond A. *Copyright made easier*, 2nd ed., London, Aslib, 1998. ISBN 0851423930

13. Useful organisations, addresses and web sites

Authors' Licensing & Collecting Society
Marlborough Court
14-18 Holborn
London
EC1N 2LE
Tel: +44 (0)20 7395 0600
Fax: +44 (0)20 7395 0660
Website: http://www.alcs.co.uk
Email: webmaster@alcs.co.uk

British Copyright Council
Copyright House
29-33 Berners Street
London
W1P 4AA
Tel/Fax: +44 (0)20 8371 9993
Website: http://www.britishcopyright.org.uk
Email: janet@bcc2.demon.co.uk

British Library Copyright Office

Boston Spa

Wetherby

West Yorkshire

LS23 7BQ

Tel: 01937 546124

Fax: 01937 546478

Web site: http://portico.bl.uk/information/cro

Copyright in Higher Education Workgroup (CHEW)

Web site: http://www.law.warwick.ac.uk/ncle/copyright

The Copyright Licensing Agency Ltd

90 Tottenham Court Road

London

W1P 0LP

United Kingdom

Tel: +44 (0)20 7631 5555

Fax: +44 (0)20 7631 5500

Email: cla@cla.co.uk

Web site: http://www.cla.co.uk

The Copyright Licensing Agency Ltd

CBC House

24 Canning Street

Edinburgh

EH3 8EG

Tel: 0131 272 2711

Fax: 0131 272 2811

Email: cla@cla-edinburgh.demon.co.uk

Design and Artists' Copyright Society

Parchment House

13 Northburgh Street

London

EC1V 0AH

Tel: 020 7336 8811

Fax: 020 7336 8822

Email: info@dacs.co.uk

EBLIDA

EBLIDA (European Bureau of Library, Information and Documentation Associations) is an independent non-governmental and non-commercial umbrella association of national library, information, documentation and archive associations and institutions in Europe. Subjects on which EBLIDA concentrates are copyright, culture, telematics, Central and Eastern Europe, information society related matters and information technology.

Ms Teresa Hackett, Director

PO Box 43300

NL-2504 AH The Hague

The Netherlands

Tel: +31 70 309 0608

fax: +31 70 309 0708

Web site: http://www.eblida.org

Email: eblida@nblc.nl

European Copyright User Platform

One stop shop for European copyright developments now continued by EBLIDA

EBLIDA secretariat

PO Box 43300

2504 AH The Hague

Netherlands

Email: ecup.secr@dial.pipex.com

Web site: http://www.eblida.org/ecupl

European Fair Practices in Copyright (EFPICC)

EFPICC is a campaign to higlight the serious concerns of leading associations independently representing European consumer, library, archives and documentation centres, disability, education, and consumer electronic industry interests about the proposed Copyright in the Information Society directive. Details of press releases and position papers are available on the EBLIDA website at http://www.eblida.org/efpicc/efpicc.htm

HMSO Copyright Unit

St. Clements House

2-16 Colegate

Norwich

NR3 1BQ

Tel: 01603 621 000

Fax: 01603 723 000

Website: http://www.hmso.gov.uk/copy.htm

Email: enquiries@hmso.gov.uk

Imprimatur Services Ltd

Marlborough Court

14-18 Holborn

London

EC1N 2LE

Website: http://www.imprimatur.alcs.co.uk

Email: imprimatur@alcs.co.uk

The IMPRIMATUR (Intellectual Multimedia Property Rights Model and Terminology for Universal Reference) project closed at the end of 1998, but its work is being carried forward by Imprimatur Services Ltd

The Irish Copyright Licensing Agency (ICLA)
Irish Writers' Centre

19 Parnell Square

Dublin 1

Ireland

Tel: +353 1 872 9202

Fax: +353 1 872 2035

e-mail: icla@esatlink.com

The Library Association
7 Ridgmount Street

London WC1E 7AE

Tel: +44 (0)20 7250 0500

Fax: +44 (0)20 7250 0501

Offers free advice on copyright issues to LA members.

Email: info@la-hq.org.uk

Web site: http://www.la-hq.org.uk

Library Association Copyright Alliance
The LACA is the main UK voice speaking on copyright on behalf of the library and information profession. It represents organisations such as ASLIB, the Institute of Information Scientists, the Library Association, SCONUL and the Society of Archivists

c/o The Library Association (as above)

Web site: http://www.la-hq.org.uk/groups/laca/laca.html

The Newspaper Licensing Agency (NLA)

Lonsdale Gardens

Tunbridge Wells

TN1 1NL

Tel: +44 (0)1892 525273

Fax: +44 (0)1892 525275

Web site: http://www.nla.co.uk

Email: copy@nla.co.uk

Issues licences for organisations needing to photo-copy press cuttings.

Patent Office

Copyright Directorate

Harmsworth House

13-15 Bouverie Street

London

EC4Y 8DP

Tel: +44(0)20 7 438 4777

Fax: +44(0)20 7306 4455

Web site: http://www.patent.gov.uk

Publishers Licensing Society Ltd

5 Dryden Street

Covent Garden

London

WC2E 9NW

Tel: +44 (0)20 7829 8486

Fax: +44 (0)20 7829 8488

Website: http://www.pls.org.uk

Email: info@pls.org.uk

World Intellectual Property Organization

PO Box 18

CH-1211 Geneva 20

Switzerland

Tel: + 41 22 338 9111

Fax: + 41 22 733 5428

Email: COPYRIGHT.mail@wipo.int for copyright matters. A more comprehensive list of WIPO email addresses is available at www.wipo.org/eng/newindex/contact.htm

Web site: http://www.wipo.org

Discussion lists

CNI-COPYRIGHT

The CNI Copyright and Intellectual Property Forum (CNI-COPYRIGHT) is hosted by the Coalition for Networked Information

Send email to listproc@cni.org

Subscribe CNI-COPYRIGHT Firstname Lastname

ECUP copyright discussion list

The European Copyright User Platform copyright discussion list is moderated by EBLIDA. It is funded by DGXIII/E-4 and forms part of the European Copyright Focal Point. To subscribe to the ecup list

send email to majordomo@kaapeli.fi

Leave the subject-field blank. In the message type only subscribe ecup-list

An archive of the ecup-list is available at www.kaapeli.fi/hypermail/ecup-list

LAW-IPR@mailbase.ac.uk (list for the discussion of UK and European issues in Intellectual Property law, with special reference to the impact of information technology and the Internet)

Send the following message to mailbase@mailbase.ac.uk:

join law-ipr Firstname Lastname

LAW-WWW

This is a list for UK academia to notify one another of new WWW sites in law, to share hints on writing better web pages, to make known new aditions to existing web pages and to discuss law-web related issues such as crown copyright, avoiding copyright pitfalls in electronic publishing, etc.

To join law-www send the following command

join law-www firstname(s) lastname

as the only text in the body of a message addressed to mailbase@mailbase.ac.uk

Linkmail (ALCS)

To subscribe to linkmail send the following in the body (not the subject line) of an email message to Majordomo@alcs.co.uk

subscribe linkmail

Newsgroups

There are a number of newsgroups dealing with copyright. These include:

misc.int-property which is a discussion about intellectual property rights and tnn.law.copyright which is a discussion about copyright law

Other resources

The Bulletin Board for Libraries (BUBL) maintains a set of useful links to web pages about copyright. These can be accessed on http://link.bubl.ac.uk/copyright (accessed 13.3.2000)

There is also a useful set of links at http://www.yahoo.co.uk/Government/Law/Intellectual_Property/Copyrights/ (accessed 13.3.2000)

A regular column called LISLEX: legal issues of concern to the library and information sector which was devised by Charles Oppenheim and associates, appears in the *Journal of Information Science* on an ad hoc basis. The *Journal of Information Science* is published for the Institute of Information Scientists by Bowker-Saur (http//www.bowker-saur.co.uk/service/ (accessed 13.3.2000) ISSN 0165-5515.

The *Library Association Record* also covers copyright issues from time to time. There is often a page with the heading 'Copyright news'; and occasionally there is a section headed 'Q&As' in which Sandy Norman answers people's copyright questions.

Edward Barrow's unofficial Internet copyright pages (Edward works for the CLA). http://www.plato32.demon.co.uk/Edward (accessed 13.3.2000)

TALiSMAN's collection of copyright links – 'Copyright and the web: online resources' http://www.talisman.hw.ac.uk/Tman-Events/old/copyright/resources.html (accessed 13.3.2000)

Aslib Know How Guides

Assessing Information Needs: Tools and Techniques
CD-ROMs: How to Set Up Your Workstation
Copyright for Library and Information Service Professionals
Developing a Records Management Program
Disaster Planning for Library and Information Services
Effective Financial Planning for Library and Information Services
Email for Library and Information Professionals
Evaluation of Library and Information Services
How to Market Your Library Service Effectively
How to Promote Your Web Site Effectively
Information Resources Selection
Installing a Local Area Network
The Internet for Library and Information Service Professionals
Intranets and Push Technology: Creating an Information-Sharing Environment
Job Descriptions for the Information Profession
Knowledge Management: Linchpin of Change
Legal Information – What It Is and Where to Find It
Legal Liability for Information Provision
Making a Charge for Library and Information Services
Managing Change in Libraries and Information Services
Managing Library Automation
Managing Film and Video Collections
Moving Your Library
Performance Measurement in Library and Information Services
Preparing a Guide to Your Library and Information Service
Project Management for Library and Information Service Professionals
Researching for Business: Avoiding the 'Nice to Know' Trap

Strategic Planning for Library and Information Services
Teleworking for Library and Information Professionals
World Wide Web: How to Design and Construct Home Pages